My Nia My Purpose

Darryl E. Lawson

CONTENTS

Preface..i

Dedicated to My Parents..iii

Chapter 1 1

Chapter 2 10

Chapter 3 16

Chapter 4 24

Chapter 5 33

Head To The Sky..40

Chapter 6 44

Being Right Hurts Sometimes 51

Get Over It Already...53

Chapter 7 56

Chapter 8 64

Silence Is Not Always Golden 71

Chapter 9 73

Chapter 10 81

Chapter 11 86

Medication 92

Chapter 12 96

Double Edge Sword... 105

Before You Let Go 108

Chapter 13 111

Chapter 14 115

Chapter 15 119

Chapter 16 125

Chapter 17 128

A Three-Ringed Circus..132

Chapter 18 133

Chapter 19 137

Chapter 20 140

Chapter 21 145

Chapter 22 149

Not That Type of Connection...152

Chapter 23 153

Reflection 157

Chapter 25 159

Chapter 26 163

Chapter 27 166

Chapter 28 171

Whose Business Is It...174

Chapter 29 175

Mirror To Her Soul...179

Chapter 30 181

I Can't Speak For You 184

Chapter 31 186

Chapter 32 189

Chapter 33 193

PREFACE

In my most humble opinion, the most difficult part of any journey is not always the first step but rather where the last step would lead one. The unknown from where a journey begins can paralyze the mind, body and spirit. Where the journey comes to an end, it can put the entire experience into perspective.

I did not hesitate to begin my lifelong journey of raising my daughter, Nia. My belief was that I was best suited to take care of her. It was not until I won custody of Nia did I think about how the journey would end. I did not know what I got myself into. There was no way of discovering how our lives would turn out or would live up to my responsibilities of a single father. There was no clear roadmap to lead me around all the obstacles that would lay in wait for me, but I would rest on my faith, trust in the Lord, and not stray from his path.

Many people use ubiquitous phrases to state that all is possible in Christ. There might come a day when a man can have a baby or man could fly without any help. Man is continually trying to enter into a realm in which he could never reign supreme. The many nights I cried for a miracle that would make my daughter normal failed to produce the results that would have pleased me.

It took years for me to see things from another perspective. Maybe Nia's disability was meant to occur. Maybe her struggles are just a part of the Master's plan for those who profess to love and care for her. Maybe it is we that should learn the meaning of life from her.

DEDICATED TO MY PARENTS

Reginald B. Lawson
And
Rhoda B. Lawson

CHAPTER 1

Slowly does the night creep away. My deliberate rise to greet the day ended with the realization that another sleepless night brought me. My state of mind was such that being late did not bring an immediate adrenaline rush that would have propelled me out of bed. It was early in the school year, and already lateness brought the possibility of a letter being placed in my personnel file. The specter of the potential blight for my pristine record did not move me to action. I conceded to myself that I must face the consequence of being late this day rather than endure another frenzied rush to exit my apartment to arrive late to work, anyway. I wanted to dive back under my covers because once on my feet, it would be another sixteen hours until I would have the opportunity to return.

I managed to make it as far as the edge of my bed, very hesitant to place my feet on the cold floor because of what might happen. My customary back woes made getting out of bed most mornings a chore. Sitting perched on the edge of my bed was my opportunity to convince myself that standing up would not be as painful as usual. My back woes were another constant in my life for which I had to learn to adjust. I was not yet forty years of age, but for half my adult life I suffered from bouts of debilitating back pain. My long-term chiropractor, Dr. Rudy, attributed my back pain to the level of stress I was under. The more stress I placed on myself, the more back pain I would suffer. I was unable to exorcise the stress from my life; therefore, the pain would always be there for me. I had no choice this morning but get up and deal with what the day had to offer me.

My bare feet touched the cold floor as I methodically craned my body to an erect position. If I were a building, the sounds produced by

1

my back as I stood upright would have sent the residents fleeing in the panic of an imminent collapse. To my surprise the last horrifying sounding "pop" produced by my back did not generate dramatic pain. It was average in that respect. Suddenly a wave of emotions came over me. In an instant, a single tear rolled down my cheek, closely followed by a second. I did not like to cry, but these tears were very much needed. I gingerly sat back down on the edge of my bed sinking my head into my hands. A negative thought that lay dormant for years resurfaced in my mind. After a brief struggle to suppress the invader was lost and the thought turned into words.

"Maybe I am not built for all this after all" I questioned myself. Sometimes I was overwhelmed with being a single father, and doubt walked through the front door. I would spend too much time vacillating on the issue, but at that particular moment, I did not see any hope of success. God knew the answer to my question. I prayed that he would enlighten me one day. There was no going back; I knew that much. The self-doubt lasted the time it took for the tears to hit the cold floor. I strained my swollen eyes to look over at the clock radio to see the time, however, the device was not in its usual location on the dresser. The missing device caused me to speak my anguish aloud.

"That girl has moved my clock" I shouted in frustration. I then searched for the VCR located underneath the television to the right of the foot of the bed sure the device was where it belonged. The numbers were small, and it was hard for me to read. I reached over to the nightstand for the glass of water I left there the previous night. I dipped my fingers in and dampened my eyelids. Most of the water missed my eyes and splashed on my undershirt. I focused my eyes on the clock, and my heart began to pump fast.

"I am only ten minutes behind schedule," I said of my realization of time. I promptly pulled my body up off of the bed, making sure not to move too fast, to stagger out of my room. In the few seconds, it took me to stagger toward the door I made a mental list of each learning objective that needed to be completed to get out of the apartment on time. I quietly opened the door to my room to make my way to my daughter Nia's room. Cautiously I opened her door to take a peek at my sleeping angel.

Nia Symone Lawson was five years of age, light-skinned with long dark hair. To those who knew her mother, Nia was her spitting image. To those who knew only me, Nia and I were twins. Most children look peaceful when asleep. Nia was not the exception. I thought how mischievous she could be when she was `awake and was glad to find her sound asleep. I gently closed the door and headed for the shower not knowing how true my thoughts would become in a few minutes.

As the warm water rushed over my body, it loosened my back muscles and allowed my thoughts to be uninhibited. Every action needed to achieve my goal of getting out of the apartment was planned down to the millisecond. Nothing could be left to chance because any miscalculation on my part could cause me to be late for work and Nia to miss her bus. Normally I would have stayed in the shower long enough to plan my day right into the evening. This short shower only allowed for me to plan out the morning.

On many different levels, I was a rarity in late twentieth century America. I was a Black Man with two college degrees, an educator, as well as a single father who had legal custody of his autistic daughter. These facts alone made me something of a specimen to be gazed upon through the microscope of life. Many people were impressed with my credentials. They could only guess at the hard work it took to be me each day. I was doing it, and by some accounts, I was doing a great job. As my unfortunate nature would have it, I often allowed the compliment to roll off my back choosing to battle with the "what ifs" of my life.

I gave up trying to make sense of circumstances that led to me becoming a single father. Thinking about it could only cause me more harm, therefore; it was a topic I rarely discussed with anyone in-depth. At hand were two jobs; one I had to do and the other I needed for survival. The fascinating fact about dealing with a special needs child was that it helped me in my chosen profession. I learned patience, determination, and compassion for any and all I met as a teacher of social studies in the New York City School System. Nia was never far from my mind. One of the few times in a day my thoughts focused on me was in the morning just before Nia awoke. It proved a pitiful attempt at "me-time," but that was all I could manage. I had to forego "me-time" if I wanted to achieve my mission.

I exited the bathroom, my towel tightly wrapped around my waist and was welcomed by the sight of Nia seated on the couch in the living room completely naked. A puzzled look appeared on my face as I questioned the reason she was seated on the couch naked. The puzzled look disappeared when I saw Nia's nightclothes on the floor leading from her room door to the couch where she sat. I knelt down making sure to keep a firm hold on my towel to pick up her underwear, the closest item to the door. The instant I touched the underwear the smell of urine was apparent. The strong odor oddly reminded me that she needed more water in her diet. The wet feel of the underwear made me drop it right back to the floor "In the bathroom you go, little girl," I said while pointing towards the bathroom. I continued to hold tight to the towel to make sure that it did not leave my waist. My baby made her way to the bathroom, as ordered, while I picked up each article of wet clothing. The wet clothes were placed in the bathroom sink to soak. Her wetting herself forced me to adjust my plan on the fly. Nia's accident added more unwanted tasks to my morning routine. Only a miracle could get me close to my schedule. I moved through the apartment like a Tasmanian devil in hopes of getting back on schedule. I washed Nia, dried her mattress with powder, changed her bedding, wiped down the couch and ironed her clothes in short order. My fast work left time to make our breakfast and wash the dishes to-boot. All the while I was cognizant of the all-important time. The morning was more frantic than usual, but it was the price of raising a child with Autism, alone.

Autism is a mysterious developmental disorder that strikes one out of ninety children born in the United States of America (2010). There were studies done on the possible causes of the disorder, but there has never been a definitive cause of Autism. Everything from environmental causes to the Mumps, Measles and Rubella shot (MMR) have been named the culprit by one study or another. What is known about the disorder is that no two cases are identical because science has learned that there are over one hundred characteristics of Autism.

Nia exhibited limited speech from three years of age until she reached her early teens. Even then, I had to serve as her interpreter because you had to be around often to decipher her language. Despite her limited verbal ability, she understood almost everything she was told as long as it was simple commands like:

"Pick up your shoes."

"Put your socks on."

"Put your pants on."

Anything more than that would send Nia into a temper tantrum as her capacity for comprehension would be overloaded. It would be years until she was able to process complex commands. "Go in your room and put your pants on then put on your socks and shoes."

Understanding her behavior was one major aspect of my job as a parent. If I raised my voice too loud or gave her commands she did not understand, it could produce negative behaviors in Nia. In urgent matters, I learned to choose my words and tone of voice carefully.

By the time all was said and done, we were only a few minutes behind schedule. I held onto Nia's hand tightly as we impatiently waited for one of the three elevators to arrive on the 28th floor of my Spanish Harlem apartment building *1199* to take us to the lobby. Just before we walked out the apartment, I had taken a doll from her, which agitated Nia. Another way to agitate Nia was to wait for anything. Waiting on one side of any door was a sure-fire way to produce unwanted behaviors in Nia. She showed her impatience in several ways including by jumping up and down in place. I understood that this was the first stage of her anger/frustration starting to build. There was a chance that her behavior could escalate into something much worse if the proper elevator did not quickly arrive.

I did not like the jumping up and down, but the alternative expressions were unhealthier for Nia. The idea of running away from me and screaming at the top of her lungs at 7 a.m. was a much less desirable way for Nia to express her anger. Disrobing while running and screaming was her ultimate expression of anger at that age. I tried to ignore the jumping and the screaming, however, I knew the next catastrophe could arrive at any moment. The middle elevator arrived which made my fear come to fruition.

For reasons known only to Nia, she refused to ride the middle elevator. As I watched the elevator door close, I suddenly felt Nia tug her hand from me. She tried to run away from me as she had done many times before as we waited for the elevator. Nia managed to take a few steps from me, however, I reached out to take hold of the collar of her shirt. Yes, it was an unpleasant experience for Nia, but if she made it to the end of the hall, she very well could have stripped down to her underwear as she previously managed. I would have a tough time explaining to my nosy neighbors why she was running from me, screaming down the hallway in nothing but her underwear. My hold on her collar was brief as I was able to take a firm hold of her arm to prevent her from running. While I held tightly to her arm, she was able to kick off her shoes sending them flying through the narrow hallway. I looked at my little girl in the face as I discussed her actions. "Relax yourself, Nia, before you get your feelings hurt," I demanded as I pulled her back to me. I held her tightly around the wrist as I was told to do by Ms. Sally, who explained it was hard for the child to break away when held in that manner and her advice proved correct. In the time, it took for me to steady her, the second elevator arrived and departed, which forced us to wait for the third elevator, the one to the left to arrive.

During the wait, I prayed to God for the strength to keep my composure and not beat the hell out of her in the hallway. When the third elevator finally arrived, the door opened, and for some reason, I did not keep a firm grip on Nia's wrist. She pulled away from me again. This time she darted straight into the empty elevator car. Her body slammed into its side with a huge thud. I quickly followed behind her with shoes in hand to prevent her from doing any more harm to herself. Feelings of anger and frustration registered prominently on my face. I looked up to pray for more strength when I discovered our private moment was made public through the camera mounted on the elevator wall. My facial expression changed, as I did not want to give anyone watching only half a story. Although my facial expression changed, my need for prayer was real, as were its results. Whenever I asked God for something, a test soon followed. I was in the middle of a test that I did not want to fail. By the time the elevator reached the lobby Nia's shoes were back on her feet, and she was no longer screaming at the top of her lungs. Her behavior early in the morning frayed my nerves more than usual. The presence of the camera on the elevator would not deter me from my taking swift action if Nia let out one scream or pulled up her shirt exposing her chest (another show of anger) but I kept my cool.

The instant we exited the elevator I realized an added reason for the temper tantrum in the elevator. Nia had a habit of walking with pieces of paper in her hand. It did not matter what the paper was just as long as it held her attention. The paper could be as large as a page from a magazine or as small as the page numbers: I reached into my bag and gave Nia a circular from Staples. It at once silenced her whining. I then led the silent girl out of the building as if we were shot out of a cannon. The cool fall air of September greeted me with chill bumps all over my arms. The blast of air caused me to pause like a statue in the park as I contemplated going back to my apartment to get Nia's jacket. Time would not allow for a return trip to the apartment; therefore, I pushed on toward the bus relying on the weather report of a warm afternoon. We made our way to the half-moon shaped driveway of the building that included the 1199 complex to see that Nia's mini-school bus was parked at the curb on First Avenue some sixty yards away. I took a tight hold on Nia's wrist and sprinted in the direction of the bus afraid that the bus would leave without her. The thought of Nia being left behind weighed on me until the doors of the bus opened. Nia laughed the entire run to the bus because she got a kick out of the excitement of running for a bus and not away from me. The anger she displayed in the hallway and elevator could disappear in an instant. Her laughter did not stop until we stood in front of the open door. "I was just about to leave you." The driver of the bus announced as we approached. The driver's sexy voice always did something for me. She was a Hispanic woman who looked as if she could be my age or younger. We often shared words in the morning. I sometimes wondered if she were just being friendly or thinking naughty thoughts. The bus matron exited the bus, and I handed Nia's book bag to her. "Sorry about being late. I had a long morning." I apologized. I looked through the windows of the minibus to wave at the three female paraprofessionals who ride with their students on the bus. Nia could be seen taking her usual seat, and I was about to leave when the bus driver asked me a curious question.

"I saw someone the other day that looked like you. Do you have any brothers?" said the driver in her rich Spanish accent.

I pondered a sly response but with time being all-important chose a simple comeback. "Nah, sweetie. I am the youngest of four, and I am the only boy."

"That's a shame man."

"Why is that such a shame?"

"I was hoping there was another one like you for me."

"Sorry to disappoint" I said as I looked at the three bus paraprofessionals whose faces seemed to echo the sentiments of the driver.

"Any word on the change of pick-up time?" I asked the driver with crossed fingers.

"No word yet mi amour." She answered with a broad smile. She then closed the doors as I watched, and the bus left.

The departure of my child did not stop me from thinking about the comments made by the bus driver. I heard those type of comments my entire adult life. It was nice when someone shared their admiration with me, but the comments rang hollow with me. "If I were *All That*, I would not be married and yet alone" I muttered as my sojourn to the subway began. Most New Yorkers like me used public transportation to get to work because the downtown areas in all five boroughs were a nightmare to drive and park a car. I enjoyed the train because the walk to the subway served as a detoxifier for the long mornings and nights. I was able to reflect on events at home and events that would occur at work. I crossed Second Avenue and replaced the last thoughts of this hectic morning with the notion that I would have to wash all of Nia's soiled clothing, no matter what time we returned home. My thoughts slowly changed from my home life to my duties as a high school history teacher and Dean in the New York City School System. My primary job, taking care of Nia, made being a teacher in a wild school seem tame in comparison.

Headlines in the local papers echoed the sentiments of many of the prominent citizens who looked disparagingly upon the teaching profession. It was a time when teachers were made the scapegoats for the ills of public education. Teaching was considered an easy job, where working only six hours a day was viewed as luxurious. If the truth was going to be told, the workday never ends for a dedicated teacher. Grading tests, creating tests, creating projects or planning lessons takes far more than six hours a day to do correctly. Often my colleagues would stay late without pay to finish the work that could not be completed in the school day. They often took uncompleted work home to finish outside of work hours. As for me, my day job of teaching and my all-day job, dealing with Nia meant I had had very little downtime.

I had reached the train station when I remembered I did not return the phone call of a concerned parent. She was more upset with her child being suspended for cursing out a teacher, two safety agents and one of the assistant principals than she was of his passing only four classes in two years. Descending the stairs to the Number 6 train closed the door on my hectic morning and opened the door to a hectic rest of the day. Some of the students I taught had the ability to do better in school, but they never knew how well they had it or they would have done better. It was my job to get as many of my students as possible to do better.

CHAPTER 2

Forty-five minutes after I boarded the number 6 train at 110th Street and Lexington Avenue, I wearily entered the doors of the century-old building that housed Chelsea Vocational High School. Students at Chelsea had the opportunity to take college classes, as well as electrical classes: that could ultimately lead to a career as an electrician making up to $63.00 per hour. The long commute followed by the long walk from the train did not allow for any recuperation time from my nap on the train. The building constructed in 1899 as an elementary school, looked every bit of its one hundred plus years. Obsolete *DC* lighting fixtures made the appearance drab and unappealing to the senses. The dull paint scheme added to the bleak appearance. The building was out of date during the Kennedy Administration, but there was no way to improve the conditions short of leveling the building. The irony is that I visited Chelsea for my first interview as a teacher, and I turned around and left the building without going through the interview. Four years later, I was teaching in the very same building, and for the moment loving my experience with the students and faculty despite the early 19th century conditions.

I strolled through the front doors just in time to hear the bell toll for the beginning of the first period. Nia's morning pick-up schedule made being on time difficult. The idiots at Pupil Transportation promised change, that the matter of a new pick-up time would be resolved in prompt fashion. Timely for them was Colored People's Time. We were one month into the school year and change had not yet come. I was at least one minute late and was resigned to the fate of being persecuted for my tardiness no matter the excuse of Nia's bus time. A rapid but stealthy transition took place within me. My thoughts changed from concern about lateness to that of a stone-faced authority figure trying to keep the peace among high school teenagers. I became a Social Studies Teacher/Dean/Assistant Coach/Head Coach and an unofficial mentor to many students in Chelsea High School. Each title came with its own level of responsibilities plus pressures. Working at a "Good School" one where the students were motivated and well behaved would seem nice, but I felt like I could make a difference at Chelsea.

I made my way past the security desk, which was in the center of the lobby where School Safety Agent Nava sat each morning. She was in charge of signing visitors into the building and directing them to the proper person. From her position, she knew much of what went into the building including who was late. She knew how late I was and she had a very good warning for me. "The principal is coming down the stairs. Go up the back way." Nava spoke just loud enough for me to hear. I thanked her for the warning as I made my way to the backside of the main staircase. As I passed the front stairwell, I could hear the unmistakable voice of the principal, Mr. Houser, and see his lower torso as he descended the stairs to the lobby. His trademark black and white-winged tipped shoes were shining brightly in the dull light. The older school buildings usually used zigzag stairwells to save space, which also made it easy to use one side without being seen on the other side. The veteran principal was a dying breed of educators in New York City in the late 1990's. The days where principals had to work their way up a long ladder to get the job were fast coming to a close. Within a matter of seven years, the standards for becoming a Principal in the New York City School System would be based less on experience but more on the whims of a billionaire turned politician.

Mr. Houser was engaged in conversation and did not see me stealthily make my way up the stairs to class on the third floor of the five-story building. I first had to reach the second floor where the main office as well as the room containing the time clock. On the way up the stairs, I planned the excuses if confronted about the time, but telling the truth was not a compelling enough argument for my lateness. I managed to run up the stairs until I reached the top of the landing on the second floor. There, I heard the voice of Assistant Principal Jenson coming from somewhere near the entrance to the stairwell. The presence of Mr. Jenson negated any opportunity to move my time card from "out" to "in," therefore I stood frozen wondering if I should do what was right or what was expedient. I chose the expedient and headed to my room. I would have to rely on my well-known forgetfulness to get away with not moving my time card. Providence must have been on my side that day because Mr. Jensen had his back turned to the stairwell, and coincidentally he was engaged in a conversation with a school aide in the clock room about teachers forgetting to move their time cards. I took a deep breath and continued up to my waiting students.

Halfway up to my assigned floor, I met Tonya Martin, a standout student. She knew I was late because her classroom was across the hall from my own. Tonya was just about to shout me out for being late when I stopped her by using the universal signal to be quiet. Tonya did not want to blow up her favorite teacher's spot thus she turned one of my often-used lines on me.

"Don't worry Mr. L, I got your back" the young girl whispered. "I got your back!"

I got your back was one of the many catchphrases I used on the students. It worked well because the students knew when I lied for effect. I gave her high five as we passed each other on my way upstairs. A few seconds later I made my way to the third floor and exited the stairwell right into the midst of a group of students who were not worried about attending class.

My run up the stairs with my heavy bag caused my back to stiffen. I stood silently giving the students a death stare for their abstinent behavior. Strong students go to class on time; weak students wait for the late bell to toll before they make their way to class; and poor students wait to be told to go to class. It was my job to make everyone move. "All of you need to get to class right now!" I commanded as I continued on my way to my classroom. Halfway down the hall, I turned around to see some students I asked to go to class still standing around, talking about nothing. I turned to walk back to the tardy students when they decided to scatter rather than hear my mouth. I continued to my class anticipating that my students would be acting wild due to my absence, which would give me the opportunity to 'light-them-up'.

I walked straight into room 325 and dropped my heavy knapsack onto my desk just as the late bell rang. I was amazed to find the students were seated quietly, waiting for me to arrive. They knew the drill about acting out when I was late or absent from school. The instant the bag hit the desk I was peppered with non-educational questions from the students.

"How come you are late Lawson" Wilson asked. He was a 17-year-old sophomore, who didn't much care for getting to school on time himself. I had an immediate response to his question. Despite its location in lower Manhattan, many of the 1,400 students were black and Hispanic and from all five boroughs. "I was captured by aliens - I escaped ten minutes ago" I jested. After a brief chuckle from half of the ten students present from a roster of twenty -five. I told them the truth about Nia's bus. As I unpacked my belongings I commented on the poor attendance. "Where's the rest of the class?" Monica Jones the star of the class answered my foolish question. "You know most of them will be here late, just like you have been lately." I knew better than to argue the obvious; therefore, I began to write the day's lesson on the board in the form of a question called an *Aim* and the motivation called the *Do-Now*. These exercises were intended to get the students focused on what they were expected to comprehend in that day's lesson. The students got to task and I went about organizing my thoughts about the best way to assess their knowledge of Ancient Egypt without giving them a test. At that moment, Mr. Marini showed up at the classroom door. He was the Assistant Principal of Pupil Personnel in charge of all the adults and students in the building.

Mr. Marini first peered through the window of the classroom before he opened the door with his master key. He stuck his head into the room, looked at me then, checked out what was written on the board the closed and locked the door without saying one word to the students or me. It was clear he had no idea I was late. This was an obvious I gotcha' moment. I believed that my job was safe for the current school year because I held seniority over all but three history teachers now in the building. However, there was a real possibility that

I could be excessed at the end of the school year, meaning there was an excess of teachers in my subject area the following school year. It was a feeling I had, based on how the principal treated me. The issues I had with the school had not gone unnoticed by my students. "Why are they sweating' you so hard Mr. Lawson?" "They're sucking you hard." Wilson articulated himself in the best street vernacular of the day. I felt the same way, but I could not express my feelings. I also could not allow Wilson to speak street language in class. Consequently, I corrected the choice of words and once again impressed upon the students a need to speak one way in school and another way with their friends outside of school. No sooner than I corrected Wilson, Stephanie voiced her opinion on the matter. Stephanie was the first of ten students I would eventually teach with the same first and last name. She was soft-spoken bright and very likable as a person. "They act like you are not a good teacher. That is the fourth time he peeked in here on you in the last two weeks" she said in a calm tone of voice. Her statement caught me off guard because I had no idea what she was talking about. Stephanie was happy to fill in the blanks for me. "Mr. Marini peeks through the door when you are too busy teaching to notice."

One of my greatest assets was that I taught more than history. I spoke to the kids about life, even if the topic was very personal to them and to me. "I can't change their opinion of me. All that matters to me is what you all think of me." There was a quick pause, then the most aloof student in the class chimed in with his own perspective. Jonathan was in his second year as a sophomore, he was clearly on the six-year plan but he was never a behavioral problem. "Your class is the only first-period class I've attended in three years in this school." Jonathan proudly stated as he completed answering his *Aim* and *Do-Now* in his notebook. He rarely took part in class, often preferring to sit and quietly observe others; therefore, his words carried much weight with the class. I appreciated the support but he was not the main focus of the day. "Don't worry about me I can handle my business very well. There is a Regents Exam in Global History four months from today that all of you must handle. If you care anything about me pass the test. That will show them how good a teacher I am."

I made my rounds to check who completed their previous nights' homework as well as the *Do-Now* on the board. It took most of the period for my anger to subside as I thought about the best ways to ditch the idea that I had a bullseye on my back that one week of late arrivals had not caused. My gut told me I was on the 'shit-list'. I vowed that day to straighten out Nia's bussing mess before I lose my mind and say things I could not take back. There were forces at play threatening my vocation, but all I could control was my home: however limited my control maybe. My love for my career choice was strong, but my tolerance for being a scapegoat had reached the tipping point.

CHAPTER 3

Eleven years in the teaching profession and much of the job was basically the same as it was when I nervously stood in front of my first group of obnoxious teenagers bent on winning a battle of wills. The changes that took place in me as a teacher were in my confidence in my knowledge of the material as well as my ability to impart information in a way relevant to all level of students. My methods were not cutting edge, filled with the use of the newest technology of the day, but I managed to get results needed by the students to succeed on many levels.

I was not the type of teacher that principals would joyfully parade in front of VIP guests, who wanted to pretend to understand what it was like to educate kids in the largest most diverse educational system in the country. I didn't look the part of a typical educator nor did my New York accent allow me to sound the part. I was proud of how far I had come as a person and was happy with myself; however, I understood very well the true nature of education and getting better meant never being stagnant. Change came slowly for me, but one thing that did not change was how students reacted to the toll of the bell marking the end of class. The students reacted to the bell in such a conditioned state that Pavlov would have applauded them from his grave. Seemingly in unison, they packed their school bags to make a hasty exit to the next class, which was the third period. Needless to say, half of them would be late for their next class and the Dean on duty would have to corral them back into class. I also reacted to the sound of the bell by taking several seconds to clear my thoughts on the morning's happenings, both in and out of the class. My eventful morning had drained me of energy.

I was able to catch my second wind in the middle of the class, finally pushing the morning events aside. The bell marked my transformation from teacher to Dean, my second such transformation of the morning. "Aims" and "Do Now's" made way for all matters of discipline. Being a Dean presented the most stressful part of my workday. In some American school districts, the position of Dean encompassed academic issues. In the New York City School System, the Dean was charged with student discipline. Being a Dean was not the type of assignment many teachers wanted, because not many were equipped to handle the demands of the duties. Breaking up fights, preventing fights, dealing with irate parents and staff were some of the duties expected of the Dean. The job of Dean was a huge adrenaline rush to which I quickly became addicted. I enjoyed the energy needed to break up fights or prevent them. The excitement caused my blood to flow as if I were once more competing in an athletic event. Being a Dean also allowed me the freedom to move around the building, making it easy to pick up gossip that would be used to defuse future events in the building. The position fed my desire to help others and deflected my inability to make sense of my daily struggles. The moment I returned from my thoughts, I realized that my help was needed.

Monique came into my line of sight. She made her way towards the door in an unusually slow manner. Her poor posture and sorrowful facial expression revealed to me that something troubled my favorite student. (Don't get mad, every student was my favorite student, some more than others.) I scanned three days of memories of Monique's behavior to detect a mood change in her. I was concerned and wanted to know if there was a problem. "Monique, don't leave. Let me holla' at you for a second." I projected in a strong voice as I waved her over to my desk. I often used unprofessional language with the students when I was going to talk with them from the heart as a means of disarming them. I was aware that I sounded corny, not serious. Monique was close to the door when I called her to my desk. She turned 180 degrees to make her way back as if I were her parent asking her to complete an inconvenient task. She huffed and puffed all the way to me. I gave her a second to collect herself before I started probing her emotional state. "I noticed you have not been acting like yourself lately. What's going on with you?" I asked as I placed the still unchecked papers back into my bag, along with the work I collected from my first two classes of the morning. Monique broke eye contact to stare at the ceiling. She began to tap her foot on the floor as an obvious sign of distress. Her eyes appeared to be puffy and red as if she cried them dry before coming to school. Monique's tearless cry provided more proof that something was wrong in the young girl's life. The sudden display of emotion caught me by surprise. I did not expect that much emotion from such innocuous questions. I stopped my actions and gave my full attention to Monique. I needed to know if her issue was a "teenaged serious" problem or a legitimate problem before I would continue. "Sometimes things are not as bad as they may first appear Monique." I spoke in a stern but matter of fact tone of voice. Monique didn't respond with a single utterance, only more huffing, puffing, and angry foot tapping.

Once again conventional wisdom was tossed aside. I tried to coax the young girl into revealing her troubles. A few seconds of silence passed before Monique finally produced her thoughts. "There is no help for me. My life is over!" Monique fatefully cried. The pain in her voice suggested impending doom awaited her. The phrase she used, "My life is over," should have been a game changer for me. Protocol dictated that at that point of the conversation, I should have stopped the dialogue and whisked the hysterical girl to her guidance counselor to have a trained professional continue the session. I would be covering my ass in the event that a dark incident would occur. I knew Monique well enough and was not convinced that she faced anything more than a "teenaged serious" problem. I wanted to probe further before I took her to the counselor. "First thing you need to do is stop all the drama, Monique. You will make yourself sick." I used a little psychology to get her to stop crying. took a tissue from out of the desk and presented it to her. Her eyes were dry but her nose was running. She pulled herself together long enough to be able to answer questions coherently.

"Is it a school problem or a home problem Monique?"

"It's a home problem, Mr. L."

"Is it something you feel comfortable talking to me about?"

"I don't think talkin' to you or anyone will help."

"You never know Monique." Give it a try," I said, paused then asked the next question on my checklist.

"You ain't in trouble are you?" I placed emphasis on the word trouble in a humorous way. I overheard Monique say she didn't have a boyfriend. Monique quickly picked up on my implication and responded definitively.

"No, neva that Mr. Lawson. I ain't crazy." She chuckled as if to say that would never happen. The pointed question sobered her up and allowed her to explain why her life was over.

Monique's life was over because her family was set to move from New York City to Georgia, before she would graduate in June. The possibility of starting over at a new school in her senior year was more than she could handle. I listened quietly, making sure to nod my head at the proper moment to encourage her to continue to speak freely. When Monique finished telling her sad tale, I asked some very important questions of Monique. "Have you talked to your parents about how you feel about the move?" I asked just as the late bell rang over the loudspeaker indicating that I was late for my patrol. I led Monique out of the classroom to the empty hallway. I needed to get to my office and she had a class to attend. It was while we were in the hall that she was able to answer.

"No. Mr. L" she responded as if the notion of talking to her parents about her feelings was a foreign concept. Her response caused another pointed question from me.

"When will the house be finished in Georgia, Monique?" "The house will be finished in the middle of April." "That's when my father will move down." "My mother, me and my little sisters will move down once my mother can find a job there."

Monique was finally able to get a hold of her emotions as she spoke. The drama had mercifully ended but the look on my face caused her grief. The exacerbated look I displayed brought about a sense of OMG fear in Monique. The only time she saw me with the same look on my face was when another student told me to "Suck his dick" and I got ghetto with the student, informing the student that I did not perform miracles. (Today I would not dare respond in that manner.) She waited for the explosion, however, what she received was something unexpected. "You jive-time super-sized dummy." "You have stressed yourself out all this time without having all the facts." My famous sarcastic response caused Monique to realize that her situation was not a grave one. I gave her another tissue to wipe her nose before I continued to console her. "I am sure if you speak to your parents they can find a way to let you stay in New York City for two months until you graduate high school." Monique heard the proverbial bell go off in her head and she had a solution to her problem. "My mother's youngest sister just had a baby and she needs help." "I can ask her if I could stay with her until the summer."

Monique's voice was filled with excitement, as the idea of staying in New York became a real possibility. I finished placing my papers in my bag as I continued to encourage her to be positive. "Are you sure your aunt could use the help provided you do not cause her any added stress, Monique?" "Her son Randy is bad and I am the only one in the family that can put him in check" she said, boastfully. I placed my bag on my back before I completed my thoughts on the subject. "You might be able to solve two problems at the same time. "Make sure you first talk to your parents," I implored. I didn't want her to cause a real problem at home by going outside the house for advice. I reached into my bag for a paper and pen to write Monique a late pass. "Let me know how your talk with your parents goes," I said as we arrived in front of the Dean's office. She thanked me then scurried to her class late, but with an excuse. I headed to the Dean's office to drop off my bag and pick up my radio to start my hall patrol.

I placed the key in the office door with the thought of how frantic teenagers like Monique could drive adults' crazy, by not thinking things through. I dodged a bullet because had Monique's situation been terrible, I would have overstepped my status and could have been called on the carpet, which would have made getting rid of me easier. I opened the door to the office and stumbled onto a powerful pow-wow taking place. The Head Dean and Mr. Houser huddled over the latter's desk poring over papers. Anytime those two got together they were dealing with a serious matter that I wanted to avoid. I dropped my bag onto my desk cluttered with graded but unreturned tests, retrieved my radio and exited the office before I was acknowledged.

As Dean Lawson, I stepped into the hallway my mind still on Monique and her "My life is over" problem, happy in a morbid way that my daughter Nia would not give me the type of drama Monique just displayed. I was just a few feet from my office when I heard the voice of a female adult yelling at full throat coming from down the hall followed by a roar of student voices. I listened closely as the shouts from a female majority would mean one thing and shouts from a male majority would mean another. Running did not seem to be necessary at the moment. The halls of the school were in a "U" shape and as I approached from the connecting hallway the nature of the yelling was all too obvious. I made my way to the source of the commotion, which had several teachers and students along the corridor poking their heads out of their classrooms in an effort to find out what was going on. Just as I was about to turn into the long corridor, School Safety Agent Lisa appeared from the stairwell. She saw the direction that I was heading and did not want to deal with drama in that particular room again. "Call me if you need me Lawson" she announced as she did not leave the doorway of the stairwell. I continued on knowing full well I could turn around. I continued on my way to the source of the commotion several teachers along the corridor peered in my direction to find out what was going on in the classroom. One had to physically hold back his students who did not want to wait on a second-hand account. They wanted to be the primary source of the events taking place in the classroom. When one of my colleagues asked the same question by just mouthing the words as to what the cause for all the noise was, I shrugged my shoulders and stepped inside the class. As Dean, sometimes I had to keep information to myself I stepped into the classroom hoping to find an easy solution.

The teacher in the room was Mrs. Hardgrave, an older woman who came into the profession later in life. As far as I could tell she knew her content, the staff marveled at her skill but there was something about her personal skills that seemed to irritate students to the point they would often go to another teacher in her subject to ask for help and not her. She did not cut them any slack, but it was who she said it that was the root problem.

Ten minutes after entering the class I was able to exit albeit frazzled but still standing. The commotion in the class began over many students being unprepared for a test and escalated to the shouting that brought me to the room when Mrs. Hardgrave made the mistake of being a white female from the Midwest who used the phrase "you people" one too many times in class when addressing the actions of the students. The phrase, no matter how innocuous the speaker may think it to be, has another connotation to the listener: especially if they are Black or Hispanic. New York City was a highly charged racial environment in the early 1990's and any perceived slight by any authority figure was challenged. When the phrase was used around me I damn well wanted to know what the person meant by "You people." The students had the same right, but I wore more than the hat. As Dean, I would often find myself in awkward positions of defending people who stood for the lesser of two evils. "What they did was wrong but what you did was far worse." I did wear the hat of a truth finding policeman. I also wore the hat of a firemen trying to put-out a small fire before it turned into an infernal. Dealing with the defiance of the students was much easier than dealing with the possible miscue of the adult.

I allowed the students to vent for a moment as a means to deflate some of the anger some of them held inside. I used a pause in the barrage from the students to turn the one sided conversation into a discussion. I laid into the students about several facts; the adults in the room had their education and they had to get their education no matter what. They needed to be prepared for class each day, with a writing utensil and with knowledge: and it was the person whom with they argued who would give them their final grades. "You have a choice to make. There is only half a period left to take the test. I suggest you stop complaining and start your tests" I announced, then waited to see several students take their seats before leaving the room. I made sure to make eye contact with several of the students in the class I knew very well, the look of disbelief on their faces as I left the class followed me into the hallway. I vowed to find those students later in the day and tell them they should have their parents come in to have a talk with Mrs. Hardgrave. Security and the Deans were in her class on a regular basis and there was clearly a problem that my position could not resolve. The students felt slighted and they stood up for themselves, which is something adults want kids to do, but I felt it had to be handled in an administrator's office and not in a classroom.

"Be advised, your second floor is a 10-99!" I announced over the radio alerting anyone who knew about the commotion that it was dealt with. "You are the man Lawson" Lisa shot back over the radio. I could hear her chuckle as she spoke. I placed my radio back on my hip and climbed the stairs to the third floor then the fourth floor and finally the fifth and top floor of the building. Each time I gave the proper code over the radio. My roving all over the building was such that the School Safety Agent Sergeant Taylor, asked me to give other safety personal the chance to do their jobs. I laughed at Taylor's suggestion, she had no idea how much work served as a distraction.

CHAPTER 4

The school day came to an end at 3:45 PM without any major events occurring. Apart from chasing students out of the halls and into their classes, the day ended with very little fanfare. As soon as the last of the students exited the building for dismissal, I gave a huge sigh of relief. My mind slowly changed from being one of several adults responsible for 1,400 young people to just handling one. The reduction in the number of children I handled was not some sort of victory for me.

The transition started the moment I closed the door to the school to have School Safety Agent Jimenez lock the door to the building behind me signaling the official end of the day. She took one look at my eyes and had to comment.

"Lawson, you look more tired than usual. You need to get some rest" she said as she completed her task of closing the lobby doors. She was about a foot shorter than me; her long dark hair gave a hint to how much longer her hair must have been during her youth. I looked down at her and shook my head.

"Rest is something that I won't get until the day I die, Nava."

"That's not good Lawson. You have to find time for yourself, or you won't be no good to anybody," she responded with her straight-forward manner. I smiled because she was right. A vacation was not in my immediate future. I neither had the money nor the babysitter for Nia for me to go anywhere past the corner store.

"One day I will but no time soon," I answered as I left Nava in the lobby, and made my way up the stairs to my office. This time I was not worried about who I passed on the way up the stairs. Each stride drained more and more of the precious energy I needed to deal with my duties at home. As I made my way to my office to retrieve my belongings, I debated whether I should stay late and put the grades in the grade book or do it first thing in the morning. The moment I saw the number of papers on the desk I knew tomorrow would be another day. I was too tired to think about grading papers. There was always some work for me to complete. All I could think about was getting a seat on the train ride home. Going against my better judgment, I took the latest papers home to grade. I looked over at the Head Dean's desk and wondered what major incident the Principal had huddled over earlier. Then I remembered to write down on my calendar the day and date of the meeting with the parent I called earlier in the day. All the adults her son cursed out pledged to be present. I was done with teenagers and angry adults for the day and could not be happier.

Ten minutes after I exited the school building I found a seat on the local C train heading uptown to Harlem. The school was named Chelsea, which is a Manhattan neighborhood north of 14th Street, nearly two miles away, but was found South of Houston Street (SOHO). As Neighborhoods go SOHO was as trendy as any neighborhood on Manhattan Island. SOHO also had the distinction of being bordered to the North by the eclectic neighborhood of Greenwich Village. The proximity to The Village enabled me to see television stars, movie stars, fashion models walking around like the average citizen. As a child, I often daydreamed about the life of a star but now, looking at the appearance of some, I'd rather work for a living.

The location of the school also made for a forty-five-minute ride uptown to pick up Nia from my parent's apartment. Normally I would take a short walk to the A express train, which made the trip uptown faster because express trains make fewer stops. The likelihood that I could not find a seat on the A express on the cusp of the rush hour made me forgo my usual faster route uptown.

I learned not to bring what happened at work into my home life. The stories and exploits of the students and faculty would only be shared if the events were extraordinarily painful or funny. I dozed off with the knowledge that this nap on the train may be the best sleep I would get. Sleeping on the train was never a wise decision any time of day, violence or embarrassment could be the end result. I was not afraid. I was too tired to worry about being mugged. As I drifted off into a mouth open, head-tilted-back slumber on a crowded subway car, I felt a rare moment of peace. A sudden impulse jolted me out of a deep sleep. My head jerked into its normal position and my mouth snapped shut. I'd managed to sleep through fifteen of the sixteen stops that it took to reach my destination, including Times Square and Penn Station. Several seconds elapsed before I realized the train had come to a stop. I gathered my senses in time to see the doors of the train open allowing passengers to exit at 145th Street at St. Nicholas Avenue Station. I had just enough time to jump off the train before the conductor closed the doors.

To professional straphangers like me, missing your stop was nearly akin to snoring loudly on the train. Both brought unwanted attention from fellow passengers. I stood on the platform to watch the train exit the station headed northbound to the Washington Heights and Inwood sections of Manhattan. In the time it took for the train to disappear into the dark tunnel I was able to shake off the embarrassment of making a clumsy dash to the door. I gave a twist to my back causing the familiar "pop" which supplied relief from my awkward sleeping position on the train. Looking foolish in front of strangers was not as important as my walk to my parent's apartment.

Even before I exited the station to the street above, the strong aroma of fried fish filled my nostrils. Once I reached the last step to street level, my bloodshot eyes fell upon the long lines of A Famous Fish Market. The fish store was one of the best known in Harlem, and for that matter New York City. All through my high school years at John F. Kennedy, I would experience the same scene of long lines in all types of weather in front of the store as I exited the train station. I did not venture to join the line for fried Whiting and fries until I returned home as a senior in college. One of my regrets was that I had not waited on the long lines while in high school.

The long line discouraged me from waiting for the fish, but I did not have to wait in line for my mother's good cooking. I put the idea of fish behind me as I turned the corner onto the always-busy 145th Street and St. Nicholas Avenue. I moved past the drug dealers selling their goods openly on the corner calling out the brand name of their product at anyone who looked to be a potential customer. I did not bat an eye as patrons of the bar, so nefarious the police would not enter without backup, crossed my path to enter and exit it. There were average people like me going about their business paying little attention to what did not directly impact their lives.

A menagerie of characters so diverse that gave the city of *Gotham* its indelible soul stood about the dirty cluttered street. My only surprise was seeing a former student standing on the corner. I always greeted him, but I never shook his hand for fear that my show of brotherhood could be mistaken as a transaction. Each time I was able, I reminded him that his business was a hit-it and quit-it proposition. He always gave me the respect of acknowledging my heartfelt sentiment but this time he was too busy delegating tasks to his workers to hold a conversation.

To be honest, I was more concerned with the weather than the characters of *Gotham*. Luckily, I wore the jacket I kept at work. The cool breeze caused me to close my jacket to protect myself from getting sick and I continued to walk as I kept my eyes open for any trouble. The walk would normally take five minutes if I was in a hurry, but I was in no hurry. My mother had Nia and I knew she was in safe hands. Also, there was plenty to contemplate and a slow walk would allow me the opportunity to sort out my situation.

Despite my tenuous marital status, I continued to do things alone. I put everything second to the needs of Nia. It was as if I could no longer progress in life but was rather walking in place, seeing the same things and experiencing the same facts each and every day. I had gone to court three years earlier to gain custody of Nia but doubt waffled back into my conscience.

It seemed like years since I hung out with the *fellas* and did not have to worry about getting back to Nia. She was everywhere in my thoughts. My deep train of thought had me walk across Edgecombe Avenue, the home of Jamaican drug gangs that ruled the two-block stretch during the 1980's with ruthlessness. When I lived with my parents, I often would spend time looking out of my bedroom window facing Edgecombe to see the happenings on the street. I could look out my bedroom window to see the flash of gunfire coming from the very block. The gunfire would soon be followed by the flashing lights of the police rushing to the scene. On the nights I watched the cyclical events unfold from my perch above the street, the idea that I would reach adulthood without any of the maladies that afflicted my peers made for a lottery dream. I continued on my way to Eighth Ave, my thoughts of old days painted my mood the darkest hue of blue.

In this moment of self-doubt, I convinced myself that my dreams were never going to be reached because I had Nia. It was the best excuse I could muster, however weak. My reoccurring moment of doubt passed with the sight of the many crackheads parading around the street slowly coming down from their last high or searching for the funds for another. Their worn-down appearance affirmed the inner strength that guided me away from the tempting life of fast money and early destruction. I was not a quitter and Nia, was not a weight around my neck holding me back but someone who had to be nurtured all the day: which just slowed me down. "You can do it, Darryl," I assured myself. Boosted by my self-assurance, I held my head just a little higher as I crossed Bradhurst Avenue one block away from my goal. I reached the corner, turned right and started south along Eighth Avenue. From Bradhurst Avenue to Eighth Avenue and from 144th to 145th street stood a vacant lot that served as the backdrop for countless music videos and movies during the 1980s and 1990s. On the corner of 144th and Eighth once stood the indescribable Ponderosa Bar. It was the type of bar the patrons of the bar on St. Nicholas Avenue avoided and the police would only enter if their backup called for backup. The first night we moved into my new apartment my father came home telling of a murder in the Ponderosa. Days later there was a double shooting in the same bar.

My jealous eye spied something that made my heart sink. I stood on the corner as I watched my dream car, a Corvette, being driven up the Ave. The 'Vette was one of the sexiest production cars in the world at the time and owning one meant financial success amongst other things. My financial status made it impossible to own anything that I could not carry in two hands. Seeing that it was a young man tooling around in that car brought a sense of animosity to the surface, erasing the pep talk I gave myself seconds ago. The animosity emerged as I pondered if I would ever have the chance to own something other than what was not a necessity. I watched with envy as the young black man behind the wheel flossed in his cherry red sports car as if he was the king of New York City just as I would have, and my mood darkened. Maybe I should have sold drugs back in the days I thought as a picture of me flossing gold caps, scantily dressed women, and a brand-new Corvette flashed through my thoughts. I could I have been rich, but the thought of laying in the gutter dead helped me to shake thoughts of avarice from my mind. With one block left on my walk I could only concentrate on the present.

I stepped on the sidewalk of 143rd Street happy that my trek was almost over. I paused to look up at the red brick twenty story building, which was often confused [it] with the adjacent Drew Hamilton Projects across the Ave. As a youth, I would often defend my building from the stigma of public housing. It was not until I returned from college did I realize that one cannot easily separate oneself from the place where they lived. Americans love to typecast others and it really did not matter because in the 1980's everyone living in Harlem was viewed by the same stereotype of being poor even if you weren't. Where one lived only mattered to those trying to fit in elsewhere. I strolled up the ramp leading to the building along the way I passed several of the older residents of the building sitting near the building entrance. They carried on a long-lived Harlem tradition of sitting in front of their building while chatting away a myriad of topics. Sitting in front of the building developed into a synchronized art form in front of *310*.

Early in the day, the elderly retired people, both male and female, would park themselves near the entrance of the building. Near noon a switch would happen, and younger adults would replace the elderly. By late afternoon younger adults would be replaced by older teenagers and school-aged children some who did not attend school. This group, with a mixture of the more nefarious elements in the neighborhood, would hang out in front of the building until the early morning depending on the season smoking, gambling, and eating. I looked at the empty bench where one would usually find all manners of discarded food strewn about in good weather and wondered how long the area would still be clean. My thoughts turned from the mundane to rescuing my mother from Nia.

The number of the building was *310*, and that number could very well have stood for the usual temperature of the lobby during the summer months. The cool temperature outside brought the temperature of the lobby down to a bearable level. Usually, in the summer months, I would begin to sweat the moment I entered the lobby of the building. The nap on the train did little to silence my tired body from forcing a huge yawn, which was noticed by Shalima, a longtime resident of the building. On many occasions, we had held long conversations about the places we hoped life would take us and our daughters who were also the same age. I had long admired the light-skinned woman for her calm voice and a good heart. In all the years we knew one another, she had done nothing to cloud my view of her being a perfect lady. She always carried herself above reproach. Interestingly enough carrying babies may have saved her life.

Shalima worked at the World Trade Center when the building was bombed from below in 1993. She was at home feeling the effects of her pregnancy when the truck exploded under the building that fateful day. Six people died and more than 1000 were injured. As fate would have it on September 11th, 2001, she was at home dealing with the effects of a second pregnancy. I took friends of a friend to see the Twin Towers weeks before they fell, and I happened to see her there. I often joked with her that if she ever got pregnant again I would leave the country. Shalima held the lobby door open for me shaking her head. "Darryl, you look as tired as I do," she said as her smile lifted my mood. "You have no idea how tired I am Shalima, and I am about to start my real job with Nia." I chuckled as my voice began to crack; I had to clear my throat with a cough before I could finish the sentence. My voice cracked because those were my first spoken words in over an hour. We made our way to the elevators as we continued to commiserate about the heat of the lobby. The door to the elevator opened and several residents fell out into the lobby. I greeted those I knew before allowing Shalima to enter the elevator while I followed. The elevator door rattled and closed with a thud. The building may not have been the projects, but *310* had serious problems with the elevators all the same.

We managed to make small talk on our slow ride to our respective floors because as usual, the elevator malfunctioned stopping on all floors on the way to the top floor. The small talk about how the building had changed from the worst in terms of conditions and tenants turned to a more personal nature. "I think you are doing a fantastic job with Nia, Darryl. The Lord will bless you."

Her warm words were followed by a warmer smile. Shalima adjusted the glasses she wore. They had slipped off of the bridge of her nose and were in danger of falling completely off her face. She could not have any knowledge of the dark mood she just rescued me from. I had to respond before she exited the elevator. "God has already blessed me with Nia as well as my family, Shalima, and good friends like you" I professed to my rescuer. Shalima continued to heap praise upon me. "Not many men would be able to handle dealing with a special needs child like you have done." "It's a hard job." "God has a plan for you, just do your part." "He has your back." The elevator finally came to a stop on the 7th floor. We ended our conversation because Shalima believed her exit was immediate. The door did not open right away. There was a brief uncomfortable elevator silence until the door rattled open culminating with a thud. She exited the elevator right into the arms of her waiting child. The sight of the young girl jumping into mother's arms, as she rambled on about something that happened to her earlier that day brought a tear to my heart. It caused me to think about the type of greeting I would receive from my own child. The door to the elevator stayed opened long enough for the scene of the mother, grandmother, and daughter embrace to cause me to shake my head.

I promised God many times that I would no longer complain about my life. I continually told myself to focus on what I now had and not what I always wanted. The sight of my dream car along with Shalima being greeted by her daughter put an end to the promise, at least for the moment. The evil that is envy grasped my soul just long enough for me to feel sorry for my current state. I would never have a greeting from Nia like Shalima received from her daughter. I knew that I might never have the means to buy a car, let alone a Corvette and the train would be my primary mode of transportation but there was always a ray of "one day."

The elevator reached the tenth floor and it stopped abruptly. The car bounced up and down as if we're at the end of a rubber band. The up and down action did not scare me because I had experienced the event several times while living in 310. What made me nervous was that I was not sure if I remembered how to open the closed door. I contemplated pressing the emergency button and waiting for help but I believed escape was a possibility. I managed to open the door and realized that the car was perched between the tenth and eleventh floors. I tossed my bag out of the elevator then jumped down to the tenth floor, making sure not to fall down the exposed elevator shaft to my death. I gave my back another twist, this time there were no weird sounds. The first part of the long day was finally over but I was about to start the hardest part the moment I took charge of Nia.

CHAPTER 5

The moment I put my key in the door of my parent's apartment door, I heard Nia being yelled at from the other side of the thick metal door. She apparently did something to anger my usually calm mother. My mother's anger was reserved for the Knicks and the fishmonger who cut off the head of her porgy. The sound of her voice had a familiar ring to it. I was not about to receive the warm and fuzzy greeting Shalima had received from her child just moments earlier.

"Hey Mother, what did Nia do?" I asked upon entering the apartment. I could not look at my mother as she gave her response. "The girl has been in rare form today!" My mother's tone of voice reminded me of the anger she displayed prior to her whipping on my butt for doing something stupid as a youth. Rhoda Bernice Lawson did not take her attention off the meal of spare ribs and collard greens as she spoke to me. Avoiding eye contact with me was another cue to her anger. I removed the key from the door, closed it behind me, then made my way over to the threshold of the kitchen where I stood and listened. "What did she do Mommy?" I removed both my jacket and knapsack to place them on top of the deep freezer. The freezer was to the left of the entrance to the kitchen. My mother closed the stove and turned to give me a lengthy account of Nia's behavior that day. "Nia gave your father a hard time today." "She kept turning the bedroom light off and jumping on the bed." My mother paused to catch her breath before she was ready to continue. "She also continually stood in front of the television waiting for me to tell her to move" she stated in absolute terms. My mother walked over to me to stand right beneath my chin. Although she was much shorter than me, I would never think that I ever held an advantage. She waited for a response that was not easy for me to formulate. It was clear Nia had gotten to her in the wrong way. She wanted guidance from me on how to deal with Nia, but I could not even help myself at that-point-in-time. I knew something had to be done, however, what to be done was the dangling participle. My sisters gave my parent's very little trouble, and then there was me and now Nia.

My parents were both sixty plus years of age, my father six years older. They met in the 1960's in Harlem and remained together through thick and thin. My parents had reached a period in their lives when they should have been traveling the world, but circumstances dictated that other things would take precedence over traveling. I looked down at my petite mother and envisioned the younger Rhoda Lawson. A white Afro had long replaced the black hair of her youth and the dark brown eyes were replaced by graying eyes. I bent down to place a kiss on my mother's wrinkled wet forehead. My kisses usually caused her to chuckle though this time she seemed not to be in a very positive mood. "I will look into getting some behavioral management for her as soon as possible." My response did not satisfy either of us. I was about to ask about my father to change the subject when Nia appeared from the back of the apartment giggling uncontrollably. Her giggling was a sure sign that she was up to some mischief.

After a long day, the last thing I wanted was more complications but that is what I experienced. I took a single step back from my mother to poke my head into the living room to see that Nia held a metal wire hanger in her right hand. Normally holding a metal hanger would not have presented such a high risk, but Nia did not understand the purpose of metal hangers. "Give me the hanger!" I loudly and deliberately ordered. I made sure to pronounce each word slowly and clearly. The unexpected sight of me caused Nia to freeze in place, and the bass in my voice made her large eyes to stretch nearly out of her sockets. Despite her petrified state she managed to let out a nervous laugh as she approached me, the instant I was able to remove the hanger from her hand. "I told you about putting hangers in your mouth Nia," I scolded as I placed the hanger inside the closet nearest to the door. I pointed my finger at Nia as I spoke and emphasized my words. Nia mimicked me by pointing her finger at me as she tried her best to repeat my threat. I wanted very much to pop Nia for her actions but this time I was able to use my voice to get my point across. My mother was slow to realize the object I took from Nia but when she did she had a fearful reaction. "Oh my God, I did not know she had a hanger in her hand!" My mother said in an apologetic tone. We had realized that Nia would place the hanger in her mouth and grind down her teeth. Watching another rotten tooth extracted from my child's mouth was more than I wanted to experience. My anger stayed with me as I emerged from the image of the teeth being pulled. Everyone in the family was put on notice about Nia and metal hangers. I then turned to my mother and tried to ease her conscience.

"You can't see everything she is doing Mommy, besides Nia knows better than to play with hangers".

I consoled my mother. I kept my stare at Nia as a way to display anger.

"Put another hanger in your mouth, Nia, and you'll be sorry."

I pointed my finger at Nia as I spoke. Once again Nia mimicked me, however, this time she repeated the only word she could pronounce clearly.

"Sorry."

After Nia spoke I was able to hear the faint voice of my father calling for Nia to turn on the light in the bedroom. "I am tired of you harassing my father." Take a seat on the couch and don't get up 'til I say so!" I commanded as I went to the aid of my father. Nia did as she was instructed and sat down on the couch, the giggling increased tenfold. I stood in the doorway of the master bedroom and at once understood the main reason why my father called for Nia. "That little girl is a pill." I uttered before I switched on the light to the room thus supplying much-needed light.

My parent's room was the most sun-deprived room in the apartment and without the overhead light, it would be difficult for anyone needing glasses to read. My father was seated upon the bed, his back rested against the headboard. He was dressed in his favorite light blue bathrobe and his signature black socks. His gaunt legs stretched out toward the footboard of the bed. I watched for a brief moment as my father struggled to adjust his position on the bed, dropping the newspaper on the floor in the process. While calling for Nia, my father managed to reposition the pillows placed under his legs. The pain that registered on his face while he performed such a simple task made me long for the strong father of old. My father was once the possessor of thick arms and a rotund belly. He got his weight honestly because he could cook any type of meal imaginable. On one occasion, I along with my sister Jackie complained that we wanted to go to a famous sandwich shop to get something to eat. "Wait right here I will make you something better" my father said before he rushed off to the store. He returned with cold cuts and all the rest. The sandwich he made for us that day tasted every bit as good as the local sandwich shop which he dubbed "A Lawson Special" It was a long time before Jackie and I spent money in the local sandwich shop again.

My father and my mother read the newspapers each and every day. When they were not reading the local news, my mother relaxed with a novel while my father curled up with a section of the encyclopedia. He walked everywhere and loved to listen to jazz when he was able to commandeer the radio or record player from one of his children. "What do you want me to do with the pillows daddy?" I made my way over to my father's bedside to adjust the pillows underneath his legs. While I adjusted the pillows, an important question of my father popped into my head. "What did your doctor say at the appointment yesterday?" I didn't get the opportunity to ask my mother, therefore, I asked the patient. My father did not have to think about his response.

"What more can he say, Darryl? I'm dying,"

Reginald Bernard Lawson shot back in his usual straightforward style when obvious questions were asked of him. The look on my face must have registered that his statement caused me much distress, but he was not one to build false hope. There was not going to be any miracle recovery on the horizon, therefore, I had to prepare myself for the inevitable. My father was not about to take back his words; he did choose to soften the statement "I am not planning on leaving this earth anytime soon but if your daughter keeps jumping on this bed, I will leave sooner than later." My father let out a sigh of relief as he finally found a position that did not cause pain in his legs. I took a seat on his father's vintage Navy trunk that was once used to store his coin collection. The collection was to serve as a down payment on a house in New Jersey, but skullduggery altered that plan. I moved some things out of the way that turned the top of the truck into a storage area. As I took a seat I looked up to see Nia standing in the doorway. She peered into the room and understood she was the topic of the conversation. "Yeah that's right, we are talking about you, Nia. You better stop jumping on the bed!" Nia giggled then repeated the word stop before she disappeared into the living room, hopefully to follow my instruction to sit on the couch. I turned to my father who had completed a quick but robust visual examination of his son.

My addressing Nia allowed my mask of despair to fall to the ground. The strain of the daily activities could no longer be shielded by jokes and excuses. My father could not simply hope that his son would weather the storm without interference; there was something that had to be said.

"It's time you think about giving her medication, Darryl. You cannot go on the way you are."

"I know I hafta' do something. She doesn't sleep at night."

"If you don't take care of yourself, Darryl, you will not be any good to anyone."

"I see what medication does to one of the boys in my school. He's hyper, then he becomes a zombie when his medication wears off daddy."

I spoke in an exhausted tone of voice. I looked at my father whose eyes were sharper than they have been in a very long time. The sharp look got my attention.

"Everyone needs help, Darryl. It's time you stop trying to be Superman" Reginald said as he started to fidget on the bed. He searched for that best position which would alleviate the pain in his legs and the discomfort he experienced in his back due to sitting for a prolonged period of time. His discomfort did not stop him from speaking his mind to me.

"There is not just one type of medication you can give her. If one doesn't work, try something else."

He paused in thought before he made a demand.

"Help me to the bathroom."

He extended his gaunt arm for me to take hold. My father never asked for my help and I was proud to do something for him. I grasped his emaciated arm and cautiously helped my father off the bed and onto his unsteady feet. My father helped me when I was a child and I lived long enough to see events come full circle. At that point in time, my father should have been the last person to tell another about their health. Being told that I needed to take better care of myself three times in one day was reason enough to listen, but I continued to wrestle with the idea of medicating Nia. For the rest of my visit, my father's failing health was my paramount thought.

Nia and I walked through the door to our apartment at 7 pm exactly; both of us were tired from our usual long day. Our circle was almost complete yet there was more to be done before I could lay my head down to sleep. I quickly took Nia downstairs to the laundry room to wash her soiled clothes and sheets from the morning because the foul smell could not be tolerated overnight. For once, Nia was calm enough in the laundry room to let me get the job done in short order. Once we returned to our apartment, I again played the role of Tasmanian Devil this time in reverse, which seemed to take more time than in the morning. Maybe it was the long day or maybe it was the fact that, another night it was just the two of us.

I did not get to bed as soon as possible. I decided to stay up and do as many lesson plans as I could for next week because there was no telling if I would ever have a chance to get ahead. I was able to get enough done that I did not have to plan until Thursday. Looking at the clock I noticed that it was only eleven o'clock, therefore, I chose to tackle the papers I carried back and forth for the week. By the time I was finished it was one in the morning, the usual time I went to sleep each day. I placed the completed papers into my knapsack and put it on the couch where it would stay until Monday morning then crept over to Nia's room.

I used the light from the bathroom to pierce the dark of her room to gaze upon both my heaven and my hard time. Looking at my terror slumber angelically I gained a better appreciation for all my struggles. I quickly closed the door because if the light awoke Nia she could stay up for three hours. The weight of the day firmly upon my shoulders and I was not sure how I managed to get through it but the next day might hold fewer surprises. There were difficult decisions had to be made if I were to have a semblance of a normal personal life. My upbringing was the pin that held me together.

As I lay in my bed trying to fall asleep before it was time to get up again, the events of my day rushed over me. I had to do better and be better to keep myself. I smiled to myself as I had my Al Bundy moment. I asked God when it will be my turn to have peace and prayed that tomorrow might be the day he would answer my prayers. Until he did, I was who I was Darryl, the father of Nia and had to handle my business. I ventured out to my terrace to look for a heavenly sign in the form of an answer, and then I began to wonder how the many men in my life would have handled the same situation.

HEAD TO THE SKY

Growing up in Harlem, New York during the turbulent 1970's, I was afforded the opportunity to study in the greatest social classroom money could never purchase. The 1970's was a time when the progress of the Civil Rights Movement first came to pass. More and more black people tried to separate themselves from the extreme poverty and hopelessness that the past held. They started to look to live in places that were not open to blacks just a few years earlier. No longer satisfied with the labels placed on them by the white establishment they began calling themselves things other than Negro and Colored. Attitudes among the people began to change slowly. There became a subconscious battle between those who wanted to forget the past embracing that which had long been denied to them and those who wanted to hold on to it tightly. The battle between the two groups was my opportunity to emulate the behaviors of those taking part in the fight.

From an early age, I learned the basics of right and wrong, of good and evil, of selfishness and kindness from the actions of the adults that lived on my block. All around me were people, mostly Afro-Americans from all spectrums of the American Society whose daily actions served as my personal textbooks. The individuals, who introduced me to local politicians, were holdovers from the past.

Mr. and Mrs. Bloomberg were holdovers from when the section of Harlem was a mostly Jewish neighborhood. The Blooms' were politically connected people who often brought political figures to the block. The Blooms' introduced me to a young black New York State Senator, Harold Denny, who served the Harlem community well into the 21st Century, just to name one of the big wigs they brought to the block. The Blooms' sparked my interest in politics by showing me that people of color worked in the highest levels of State government - many of the things I would come to enjoy came from living on the block.

Respect for the law came from my interaction with the police officers that patrolled the area. My mother told me early in my life "not all police are bad." "It's the man who wears the badge that is either good or bad." A chance encounter with French Connection cop Eddie "Popeye Doyle" Eagan reinforced what my mother impressed upon me. He drove through the block in an unmarked car and when I shouted out his name, Popeye stopped his car and told all of us playing skellies to stay in school and stay out of trouble. I vividly remember he looked the same as he did in the movie. I am not sure if his "Stay in School" was heartfelt or just what he was told to say but the fact that a famous white cop shouting words of encouragement and not "Get the fuck against the wall" made me respect the person not only the badge.

In the 1970's a man would give anything to own a Cadillac. It was the main symbol of wealth in places like Harlem. There were two individuals on the block that owned America's dream car (both lived along with me in 628 West 151st Street); one was a woman the other was a puzzle. Grant who lived on the third floor of my building owned a Cadillac. Grant's car was purple with whitewall tires and curb finders dangled from the sides. Grant could have been the inspiration for the R&B song "Just Be Thankful." His flashy attire consisted of mink coats, loud colored suits and wide brim hats that might have given The Knick legend Walt "Clyde" Frazier fits of envy. At one point Grant had two girlfriends, one white and the other black, both of them were stone cold foxes. The black girlfriend who went by the name of Ronnie lived with Grant the longest.

Ronnie was a slender foxy mama. As far as I can remember, she never dressed down. Long gowns and sharp pantsuits are what I remember she wore the most. Whenever she came into the building she spoke to us kids and made me want a fine soul sister like her when I was a man. Can you dig it?

Grant's car was at the classy end of the spectrum, but Timmy had the hot rods. Timmy was in his twenties and owned two muscle cars during his time on the block; a purple Dodge Roadrunner and a black Hemi 'Cuda. Those cars would make any car enthusiast giddy. He smoked the tires every chance he got when entering the block which brought him the attention he sought but did not need because the cars spoke for themselves. Many of stickball games had to be put on hold for safety reasons when he pulled either into or out of the block. His choices of cars were hip and the sounds produced when he stepped on the gas pedal were intoxicating to my ears. I vowed that my first car would make a statement like Grant's Cadillac and be as attention-getting as both of the cars owned by Timmy. Cars aside many of my other interest developed while I called that block home.

The people of 151st between Broadway and Riverside also shaped my interests in photography, sports, and John F. Kennedy High School, Bronx New York. My interest in the military came as a result of the countless helicopters that flew low over the Hudson to their base north of the city. In all the people on the block influenced me greatly, but their influence did not reach the level of influence the men in my family had upon me.

My uncles made perfect role models for me to study. I fantasized about smoking a pipe and being a smooth talker like Uncle Charlie. I wanted to be like Uncle Alfred, wild and the life of the party or like Uncle Richard: funny and yet serious in the next breath. I wanted to take excellent care of my car like my Uncle Clifford, who had the same car for twenty years. My uncles were not the only role models that affected my life.

I dreamed of being cool like my sister's boyfriend, Muskrat, or street smart like my cousin, William. Joining the military was a possibility for me due to the service of cousin Burt in the Army. I heard the stories of my cousin Justin who lost his life in Vietnam. I wanted to play basketball as well as my cousin "Butter" and I hoped for the day I would have the style and money like my cousin Charles. In spite of all the interests, there were only two people who influenced me more and one of them was my father.

It was from my father that I gained a love for history. It was he who told me that the Japanese sent balloon bombs to attack the United States during WWII. This was long before it became widely known. My father taught me about life and about how people react to certain situations. Through his actions, my father taught me not to drink and to never give up on my dreams. He gave me my light complexion, my flat rump, my laugh as well as my sense of humor. I could not aspire to be more than what I am already, Reginald Bernard Lawson's son. Not a quitter but rather a fighter: and it would take a tremendous fighter to deal with what life had in store for me. All I had to do was to keep thanking God for the family and friends for what He gave to me and would give me one day.

CHAPTER 6

My early teenage years marked an interesting period in my life. It was at this time I began to realize why some woman had round bellies and others had none. Enough babies were being born around me, my niece Vonnetta included, that I became curious and asked questions about life from the adults around me, but only in my mind. I was too frightened to speak the questions thus I only thought about them. Around that time I was tasked to pick my niece up from daycare, which provided me with the first act of responsibility other than walking the dog. My limited experience with major responsibilities made me wonder what it would be like to be a full time parent; could I take care of my future children.

By the time I reached the age of seventeen becoming a father was a real possibility. Many of my friends had already joined the parenthood club and, as a believer in the odds, I felt my membership would soon come. My behavior and attitude did not help matters. AIDS was not yet full-blown epidemic killing thousands and scaring millions more, therefore prophylactics were not yet a necessity to have sex. If my turn to be a father did come I believed I would be more than ready, I looked at my surroundings for the best attributes of a good father.

There were many men that could be used as a template for fatherhood. I conveniently took from each the quality I most admired until my ideal father became a monster out of a Mary Shelley novel. I did not seek to bring life into this world but being prepared was something I felt needed to be done. The wait to be called "Daddy" fortunately did not come too soon. By the time I entered college my attitude changed, she was not going to get love if "Jimmi" didn't wear a glove. My chance to be a parent came a decade later under circumstances I could have never factored into my plans.

When one first learns that they have helped to create a precious life many emotions may arise. Age, marital status and most importantly the identity of the other donor of chromosomes will decide what emotions may come to the surface. My long wait to experience fatherhood and the subsequent reactions to the pregnancy brought about feelings it took years to depose.

My first reaction to the knowledge that I would finally be a father at the age of twenty-eight was a total surprise. My joy increased each time I informed friends and family until I found myself in a state of euphoria. My altered state of immense pride and fulfillment slowly deflate over time. There were signs that I ignored for whatever reason, signs that could have served as a preamble to a lifetime of difficulty that was on the horizon.

There came a point during her mother's pregnancy that I began to worry about its ultimate outcome. External pressures emerged and were placed upon us by what seemed to be the entire world. The constant drip of opinions from family and others about our unborn child made it difficult to hear my own voice on the matter. The continued interference kept me up at night and had me sleepwalking in the day. My chest was tight and more than one person voiced their concern about my well-being. Those closest to me knew all my struggles to keep the vines of negative thoughts from growing. I could not determine how her mother was affected, but any level of stress was never good in a pregnancy.

Working in a school full of hormone-crazed adolescents made me want to return to a peaceful home. To my limited surprise I entered my apartment to find her mother seated at our small table with her bags packed. She looked at me with her big brown eyes and gave me the reason why she had to leave me. She was in her third trimester and the reason was not all her own. Needless to say, my thirst for relaxation would not be quenched.

I had enough of the poor advice she was not voluntarily obtaining. For one of the few times in my life to that point, I meant every word of my response to her statement. I wanted very much to speak to the author of the suggestion for her to leave in the most direct voice possible. There was no doubt that my septic tank of a mouth was about to explode spreading all type of excrement in the direction of the author of the divisive idea. Nia's mother heard my argument for her to put wax in her ears and think about what she wanted. I then asked her what she wanted to do, to stay or to go, and she gave her answer. She chose to stay. It was the last time voices tried to separate us in such a direct manner but the battle was only in its infantile stage.

In one way or another, the external pressures resurfaced to be talked out between us. My chest still hurt and my soul cried out for peace. To make matters worse, by her eighth month she suffered from regular Braxton-Hicks Contractions. Every other night the bags were packed at the door for us to run out to the doctor. I was a nervous wreck as I tried to keep calm and to keep her calm. Even when I received a call from her college telling me she was not doing well, I kept my composure during my frantic mile run to be by her side. The constant state of being on-guard took its toll on me. I grew less sensitive to the many signs of imminent birth, much to my chagrin.

"Keep ignoring me and I will have this baby in this apartment." Nia's mother told me very calmly. She stood in the doorway to the bathroom in the studio apartment we shared. The prior night we spent hours in the hospital due to another false alarm. We were sure that this was the real thing until we heard the screams of a woman inside the delivery room. The woman's visceral shouts in Spanish convinced us that we were not going to be parents that day. We looked at one another and left the hospital.

I went to work dead tired and without much of the sense God gave me. My senses were on a time delay often experienced on live telecasts. Each spoken word to me and from me had to be restated in my head in order for it to resonate with me and for my response to be coherent. I gave a quiz that day as teaching a lesson would have been very difficult. Getting home and being bombarded with fears and false alarms numbed my sensitivities.

Later that night, I peeked out from under my cozy covers to see her mother's silhouette backlit by the bathroom light. I made a quick assessment of the situation and decided that I had better listen to her.

The sight of thick clear fluid mixed with blood dangling from between her legs made her appeal relevant. They were clear signals I could not mistake as the adrenaline coursed through my veins.

In a matter of minutes, we were in a cab on our way to Columbia Presbyterian Hospital to deliver our child to the world. During the fifteen-minute ride, I remember Nia's mother was relaxed despite the occasional strike of labor pains. It was there in the cab, for the first time, I was scared for the future. I was scared for what my life would become and what my child would experience born to flawed parents like us.

The movies and television were the only sources of information about childbirth although exaggerated must have a basis in facts. Showing men excluded from the birth process was the way it was done in life and in fiction. I was all in on bucking the old ways until her mother let out a scream that had me shaking in my boots. I was pleased to find that, at least in my case, life did not imitate art.

I did not faint, pace back and forth nervously, or do any of the other stereotypical things attributed to new male parents in popular media of the day and neither did her mother. Her mother did not curse the day she met me, nor did she dig her nails into my skin and draw blood whenever the horrific labor pains struck. She simply allowed me to coach her breathing as we rehearsed in Lamaze class. Her mother let out one more powerful scream that brought the doctor into the room. It was clear that she was ready to deliver.

I saw the crown of Nia's head pushing its way out and that was all I wanted to see: too much blood and gore for my taste. Early in the process, the Labor and Delivery Nurse asked me if I wanted to stay in the room for delivery. I firmly agreed at the time but the shriek and seeing the crown of Nia's head chased my courage from the room. My body was set to follow my courage out of the room, but the Labor and Delivery Nurse impeded my path. Two steps were what I managed to take before the nurse called out to me. Her voice stopped me in my tracks and forced me to turn around and face my fear. The sight of the doctor pulling Nia out was enough to draw me back to my original location against the wall. "You were there at the beginning, you have to stay for everything" the nurse informed me as she shoved the metal table in front of me preventing me from leaving until she was ready for me to leave. Nia's birth was more exciting than I could have ever imagined.

On May 20th, 1994 at 7:52 AM, Nia Symone Lawson came into the world. [pace] I made a quick count of fingers and toes and was relieved to find all her digits in place. A feeling of pride overwhelmed me, as I was now more than just a man I was a proud father to-boot.

In my moment of exaltation, I remembered the experiment I conducted while Nia was in the womb and it was the time to test the results of a said experiment. I often spoke to Nia when she was in her mother's stomach. I read somewhere that babies could pick up on familiar voices once outside the womb. I called out to Nia as she lay on the table after she was cleaned. To my astonishment, Nia turned her tiny head in my direction! Her reaction to my voice would surprise me for the first of many times in my life. I finally had my family and happiness was mine to enjoy.

Most things in life are not how we imagined them to be, fatherhood included. I was present for the baby talk and hugs but I could not have foreseen the mental and physical energy needed to properly take care of an infant. Hard work never scared me; therefore, I dove into this massive undertaking relishing even the most mundane jobs because this may be my only chance at being a parent. I could not be sure that I would ever experience it all again.

I changed diapers, washed bottles, went food shopping, did the laundry and fed Nia too. My thinking was that her mother had done the hard part in delivering our little joy, the least I could do was take care of most else. I even took the midnight feedings because Nia's mother would have her during the day while I was at work. I hoped my actions would relieve any fears she had about my commitment to our new family. I wanted to show Nia's mother how committed I was in our relationship by putting to rest all the events in the past that kept Nia's mother from seeing a bright future for us. Hope and prayer sometimes are not enough to right the wrongs that were committed in the past.

What started out as a joyful event turned into a roller coaster ride that I was unwilling to disembark. The drama with her mama aside,

Nia became the lone ray of light in my black hole of a world. There was no hint of an issue with Nia. She progressed like every other toddler her age including her cousin Jazmine Simone who was three weeks older. Nia reached milestones alongside her cousin and, in some respects, Nia surpassed Jazmine. At seven months Nia called out letters on the television show <u>Wheel of Fortune</u>. Everything about Nia was going as it should. Each stage of her young life was well documented by the hundreds of pictures taken by me. The spark in her eyes gave no sign of the disorder brewing within her. It was not until she was one year old that the signs of trouble began to appear.

At the age of one, her speech did not progress as it should for a toddler her same age. She continued to speak the same gibberish she had uttered for months. The sparkle in her eye dulled and her smile told a story of uncertainty. Her mother was the first to notice something was not right with our child. Nia's mother recognized something was wrong, but her dark view of our world caused me to take her idea with a grain of salt. There were other things she believed she recognized that were untrue. She accused me of being broke because I spent my paycheck on other women to which I had a classic response.

"I can hardly deal with you. Why would I want to take on another headache?"

She did not believe me, continuing to insist that I was running around on her. Truth be told at the point, I wish she was correct. At least there would have been a good reason for the discord in our relationship. Fighting with her mother prevented me from seeing the obvious signs that my little girl was not progressing as a child her age should. Instead of focusing on our child, I spent my time trying to prove to myself that I was not the bad one in the relationship. As a result of a favor, I took my blinders off and stopped denying the obvious.

I asked my sister Debra and her husband Larry to watch Nia because her mother and I had an event to attend. When we returned to get our angel, Debra said she had something to tell me but it could wait until we got Nia home. My sister, reluctant to bring me bad news, spoke in a deliberate and well thought out manner over the phone.

Debra very rarely made unsubstantiated assertions and if she believed there was a problem then she had a good chance of it being based on facts, not fears. I prayed my sister and Nia's mother were wrong but deep down I knew there was a problem; my sister spoke to the common sense feeling I chose to ignore. My response to my sister was a matter of fact. "If she is special, then she is special, but I will find out for sure." Her mother insisted something was wrong with Nia. I was ignoring her concerns and she was correct. It was not until I reported Debra's comment to her that I had to admit I was wrong. She was right in a way, for I prayed that nothing would be wrong with my only child.

BEING RIGHT HURTS SOMETIMES

Immediately we sought professional help to find out what was wrong with Nia and why she did not progress like all the other children her age. The place we first looked to find answers to our burgeoning questions was Harlem Renaissance Health Center, a local health center that is affiliated with New York City Hospital System. Nia went through a full battery of tests including hearing and eyesight tests; the doctor came back with something of a unique answer for why Nia appeared to regress.

"There is nothing wrong with your daughter. Just keep talking to her she will be fine" he said as if we had come to him for a Band-Aid for a scraped knee. The doctor gave us the proper diagnosis of Pervasive Developmental Disorder, PDD for short. In medical terms, it meant that something was wrong with Nia but medical experts could not give a definitive diagnosis. I hoped that the doctor was correct in his prescription but in my life, nothing was easy. Her mother did not settle for the prognosis and this time I listened to her. We took Nia for another opinion, this time we chose a place that was known for its work with special needs children.

After another series of tests, doctors at the venerable Rose Kennedy Center in the Bronx, New York were able to give us the broad definition of PDD but a definitive diagnosis of Autism. Her mother and I were not familiar with the term and had to do some research on the new-fangled Internet to find out what it meant for Nia. Knowing was half the battle for us but knowing brought about an entirely new set of demands we were not sure of how to handle.

Autism is a developmental disorder that by 2010 affected one out of every ninety-five children born in the United States. Autism has over one hundred characteristics thus not every case is exactly alike. The disorder affects speech and social skills as well as comprehension. Repetitive behavior is also a symptom of the disorder. There was no way to know early on what behaviors would come and go and what behaviors would be ingrained in her mind. Armed with the best information we could find, her mother and I were able to temper our fears, but the cause of the Autism was the question everyone wanted answered.

I pored over articles from all sources to find the culprit for what ailed my daughter. The more I read, the less I knew about the cause of Autism. When Nia was a toddler, the prevailing thought was that Thimerosal, a mercury byproduct used to preserve the mumps, measles and rubella shot, was the catalysts. Years of extensive medical reviews show the mercury theory had been proven less likely than environmental issues as the primary cause. Whatever the causes, Autism affects mostly males and by 2016 one out of every sixty-eight children born in America were diagnosed with Autism.

Nia's mother grew up in and around tobacco fields and cornfields in South Carolina. These fields were regularly sprayed with pesticides, which undoubtedly were inhaled and ingested by her mother and her family. There are studies that point to this as a factor. Other studies claim that the sperm from fathers over the age of forty may be the culprit. If age was a factor, then why are there not large numbers of Autistic adults conceived during the Baby Boom after the end of WWII? As for me, I was twenty-eight years old when Nia was conceived so the age of my sperm should not have been an issue. Whatever the causes, one out of ninety-five children born in the United States in 2016 suffered from Autism and most of them were male.

Every day brought about new issues as we tried ways to deal with having an Autistic child. What was normal for Nia? What were behaviors we had to deal with as parents? Most of all, we had to learn to adjust our lives to fit her needs. The latter was the most difficult lesson we had to learn. No matter how many words of encouragement I received, there still remained a strong sense of dread that I tried to conceal. We did all that we could, the rest was up to the Lord.

GET OVER IT ALREADY

There are some parents of "Special Needs" children who never accept the fact that their offspring suffer from a disability. Some others need no time to adjust to the situation. For me, it took many years for me to deal with the hand fate had dealt me without pity or sorrow. By no means was the process a smooth transition. There were many peaks and valleys traversed until I found a more comfortable place to deal. To that point each day brought new situations.

I spent the first part of Nia's life worried about what others would think when Nia displayed one of her behaviors in public. I thought about how I reacted to similar circumstances when I was a youngster and there was no way I would allow my daughter to be gawked at or made the butt of jokes. My fears soon faded as my Harlem, New York attitude came out of me. The icy stare I gave many people let them know to keep their snide remark to themselves when Nia repeatedly clapped her hands or performed hand flapping. No matter my reaction I felt my anger begin to grow to monumental proportions.

Although at the time of Nia's birth I did not attend any church, but I had ongoing conversations with God. My conversation centered on my feelings, not Nia's condition. Selfishly I asked "Why did this happen to me?" and "How could I be the first person in my family to have a child born with special needs?" I was controlled by my wants and needs. My reaction delayed me asking the true questions of God about how I could have the strength to adapt to Nia's abundant needs.

It was the "WHY ME" stage that took me a very long time to get over. Every one of my friends had children. Some of them starting to produce at life at the age of 15 and all of their children were fine. I cast an envious eye at my fortunate friends who had "Normal" children who could live life to the fullest. One day the child would grow into an adult and leave the home. At one point, I thought Nia was payback for earlier transgressions including the fun I made of "retarded" children as a youth. My attitude served to deflect the words of encouragement I constantly received.

"God doesn't give you more than you can handle."

"You will be blessed by God."

"You dress her nicely," I was told with enthusiasm.

These were some of many words of inspiration bestowed upon me that were lost because I could only see the flaws in my child and not all her unique beauty. I did not know it at the time, but I actually was judging myself and not my child. The clear meaning of the words was that God saw me as a strong person able to deal with the complexities of being a parent to an individual like Nia. I wished he saw me as a punk so my child would be born without a developmental disorder with no cure and no apparent cause. My frustration over Nia was nothing like what her mother felt.

Nia's mother could not come to grips with her child suffering from a developmental disorder. I did not understand it at the time but she saw herself in Nia. It was a weird notion but in time events were explained that made sense on some level. I was a fireman again; not putting out fires of angry students but rather fears her mother conjured up. Despite my own trepidation I tried to get Nia's mother to get over her negative feelings, and get on with the job of raising our child together. Her mother verbalized what I only allowed myself to think. My issue with speaking my mind came to roost once more.

After Nia's mother departed, I found myself seated at my parent's dining room table engaged in an everyday conversation with my mother. In the middle of the conversation, I remember venting about Nia's condition and how I needed help. It was the first time I publicly expressed my true feelings to anyone. My mother sat and listened quietly without interruption until I paused for air. She looked straight into my eyes and said something that made me think. She sat up in her seat and pointed her finger at me, the one she always pointed when she was about to lay down the law, and artfully put the onus back upon me.

"Nia is your cross to bear."

Those words from my mother caused me to reevaluate what it was to be blessed as well as to be a parent. I could either wallow in pity or I could take action and make Nia's life as great as possible. From that day on I made more of an effort to enjoy my child and not dread my responsibility. I had to believe I was chosen and not cursed.

CHAPTER 7

The key to best handling a special needs child is getting them the health care they vitally need. Since I was a city worker, my health coverage was good enough to take Nia to the doctor when needed. I knew that if I had money I could seek out treatments that were available at the time. In an effort to gain such money I began to write the great American novel. My thinking was that, short of hitting the lottery, the best way of taking care of Nia was to have a great healthcare team in place. Even when she was a toddler I had my eyes set on Nia's future. While I pecked away on the typewriter, Nia needed to have a slew of doctors that would assist us in taking care of her. Nia's mother and I first searched out a good primary care physician.

As stated prior, we believed that the shots administered by her primary care physician were what triggered the Autism, however, her mother and I had no idea when we chose him. It was difficult to choose names from the book sent to me by my healthcare company, therefore, we used word of mouth to find her a doctor. When Nia was young there were not many doctors who possessed the skills needed to treat special needs children. As her parents, we wanted someone who was willing to listen to our concerns and have a great deal of knowledge in the field of Pediatrics. What we got was a no-nonsense doctor who had an interesting way of going about his profession.

The physician we chose had an esteemed practice on the second floor of a Brownstone near the famous Strivers' Row. The row of houses once built as country estates for wealthy 18th Century New Yorkers, were symbols of wealth for the current occupants. His office walls were decorated with awards including typed letters signed by important individuals in New York City History. Having a good doctor relieved some of our fears concerning what to do with Nia when she was sick. We stayed with him until he offended Nia's Mother.

Nia's mother took a dislike for the Doctor. I could not find fault with the man other than his stinging language, which did not bother me very much. I was focused on my child's welfare plus he had never said anything salty in my presence. He gave us guidance that we needed as young parents. I did not hear the man say anything considered offensive until we brought Nia into him for a recurring illness.

Nia was teething and, as often happens, a fever would develop as a result. After several trips to his office for repeated fevers, he called us paranoid parents; that comment, among others, sent us searching for another primary care physician. Our choice brought us to another recommended doctor who was the total opposite of the first.

This doctor spoke in a cool non-condescending voice, unlike the first doctor. His heavy Caribbean accent made him more like a professor than a doctor. He took time to speak to each patient, sometimes making the wait to see him even longer. If it was your turn in the examination room, then the conversation was never too long.

He was the type of doctor we needed to ease our fears of raising a child with Autism. There were many variables that a mathematician would have trouble calculating the possibilities of her behavior exhibitions. Our new doctor saw many cases of Autism: thus he could guide Nia's mother and me in the proper direction. Having a good physician was a Godsend for me. I thought that her mother would have the same appreciation for him. My chest burned with an uneasy feeling that Nia's mother would never be able to adjust to our child being who God intended her to be. I had my own doubts but as always, I kept them to myself until my feelings overflowed.

One evening, as we sat on the bed in our quaint studio having yet another conversation that should have been put to rest long ago, the spirit came over me. Nia's mother was still pregnant at the time and there was no end in sight to the doubt and fears she expressed about impending motherhood. I remember looking in her big brown eyes and uttering the obvious, according to me.

"Either you are going to grow up or you will crack up!"

I remember repeating the sentence twice to make sure she heard me. I cannot recall her response but from that point on there was no doubt in my mind that I was in over my head with Nia's mother.

The experience of being a new father was all that I hoped it would be for me. I enjoyed every aspect of my duties even cleaning soiled diapers. There were times I felt the three of us were a real family and the doubts I had about staying together were wrong. Then things would happen that made me believe staying together would drive me insane. Through it all, I continued to hope for the best and plan for a way out.

I began to look for an escape plan, but my heart would not let me leave Nia with her. I stayed to endured unbelievable tales of "what if's" which could cause a miscarriage. Then there was that thing with her aunt trying to get her to leave me. Once Nia was born, there was no way I could deny that I should have stuck to my original plan of having us go to therapy before I allowed her to move in with me. Going against my gut only prolonged disintegration of our relationship.

The impending end of us was more painful than any method of torture the C.I.A. could have devised. There was no way to avoid experiencing guilt, anger, sadness and even rage as each day came and each night brought a continuation of suppressing one emotion over the others. Arguments her mother and I had during that time over money and every conceivable activity connected to raising a child where never ending. When we were not arguing, I spent my time caring for Nia and anticipating the next topic for our heated discussion. I made the conscious choice not to enjoy my blessings: instead I chose to dwell on problems both imagined and real. I did not realize it at the time, but I allowed myself to live in a constant state of stress. Pulling away from what used to make me happy, like friends and family, was my way of trying to solve the problem I was not equipped to deal with on my own.

The stress of dealing with her mother and putting out fires time and time again took me to a state of mind I wish to have never experienced. I had become what my parents preached against. Each morning I looked into the mirror, hate filled my heart. My hatred was directed at the man in the mirror. I had allowed her behavior to give the Devil residence in my soul, turning my heart blacker with each new incident with Nia's mother.

Each thought I composed was filled with anger, never looking at the bright side of the situation. It was as if I went back in time to my elementary school days where I felt inferior to my classmates in every subject except social studies class. I did not realize then, back in elementary school that allowing anger to take hold would not help me: only hinder my abilities to see right from wrong. Work became a place where I could get away from the madness that festered within me. I lost respect for myself, and all the praise heaped upon me for the work I did with Nia equaled mud on a white suit. It would be years before I could look into a mirror and not dislike the reflection. I would never feel the same about Darryl Eugene Lawson.

In addition to looking down on myself, I was consumed with trying to find the way out of the longest relationship of my life. There had to be something I overlooked that would make Nia's mother see that her thinking process was incorrect, the more I searched for the magic key the further I got from finding that key. Everyone around me understood the pressures I was under because I vented to those who cared about me.

There was no going back to a time before my child was born, when her mother and I got along better, when we used to hold hands walking down the block or the time when we drove south to visit her mother's family. I was in hell and only trusting my prayers would pull me from the abyss. My resolve to leave came through a series of encounters with old friends. Each encounter bolstered my resolve of escaping from my unhappy home life.

Long walks, especially at night, were a means other than writing that helped me process my thoughts of the day. The demons allowed to fester within me were put to rest during those walks of solitude. I walked late in the night because walking in the daylight would have revealed to anyone who wanted to take notice that I was in a daze.

Many times, I walked past acquaintances during my walks alone because I was deep in thought only to have them literally wave their hands in front of my face to gain my attention. Sometimes my walks took place in the daylight hours, which made it difficult to hide my trance-like state. During one daylight walk, I passed a former Harlem Hospital coworker the very place I met Nia's mother. She stepped directly in my path, which brought me out of my dream like state. My former coworker was much shorter than I thus my neck craned down to look into her big brown eyes. Two physical attributes that made her attractive to me were her beautiful dark skin and her wonderful smile. I remember she had the perfect Colgate Smile, her white teeth and we had several conversations about the importance of keeping one's natural teeth. My attraction went no further than enjoying working near a beautiful woman. Her personality made her one of the most pleasant women I knew. We chatted a minute about the people we worked with and those who continued to work at the hospital, but I was anxious to get back to my walk and looked to back out of the conversation as politely as possible when she said something that caused a revelation in me. She looked up at me her dark skin gleamed in the sun and her perfect teeth were displayed through a powerful smile as she addressed me.

"Every time I see you there seems to be something heavy on your mind,"

She said as she waited for my response. My response, I do not remember but, I do remember what she said next.

"You don't look like you did when we worked together."

Her words were true. I had allowed stress to eat away at me. I lost weight to the point *crack-heads* even asked me where I got my supply. I had heard it before from others but this time I decided to admit it to myself. I assured her the next time she saw me I would be different.

"Take care of yourself. You have a child to think about" she reminded me as we parted company. As I walked away I knew she was right to be concerned about me.

Recently while on a night walk, I came upon the closed doors of the old K Building of Harlem Hospital. The building housed the psychiatric ward. I can still see the huge metal doors in my mind's eye, the street lights reflecting off them like spotlights. I could no longer deal with the stress of both the relationship and Nia. Checking myself in seemed the best call for help I could muster.

As I contemplated what I knew needed to be done, the huge metal doors were flung open and a black doctor emerged. He held the door open to take a breather from his work within. It was clear he was a doctor because the white smock and stethoscope were sure signs. The muscular man did not leave the doorway; he used his back to hold the heavy door open. Although I did not know the man, he represented all the black men in my life. My cousins, friends, and teachers, and those I worked with who I felt would be disappointed with my allowing myself to be dragged down into the depths of despair enough to seek psychiatric help. What would Levine, Ennis, Fergusson, and Mitchell think about me? The doctor took notice of me for only a short time before he returned to his own thoughts. I recoiled from the idea of going in and disappeared into the night to continue my walk. I could not be crazy because as my father always said, "Crazy people don't know they are crazy."

Thoughts of hurting myself were erased from my mind forever but I became more determined to stick to my plan to once and for all free myself and my child from the person I knew could hurt us both.

Throughout my struggles with Nia's mother, the people close to me told me that I needed to think about leaving once they began to notice a change in my personality. At first, I didn't say much about what happened in my relationship. They could see the change in me and knew I had could not continue trying to fix a relationship alone. If I left back then, there was a good chance that she would have taken Nia south with her and I would never see my child again. Nia and I were together until death we did part.

On my way to my mother's apartment to get Nia I ran into an ex-girlfriend. Ex-girlfriend is a slight exaggeration. I sweated her for years only to have her tell me she was not interested. She said that the men in her life broke her heart and she was not ready to have me [to] be the latest. We saw each other on occasion and one of those occasions I must have expressed my relationship ills to her. She was not one to hold her tongue and when I gave my tepid response to the question.

"How is your relationship going?"

She let me have an earful.

"Are you still having problems with that chick, Darryl? Hell, I could have driven you crazy in less time" she said in all honesty and she was right. I did not need the stress any longer. Everyone seemed to know that my relationship with Nia's mother was not going to bring out the best in me, only the worst. Once I got home that night, and the usual crap started, I had no choice but to end what was already dead. We soon were headed for Family Court for a custody fight over Nia. The prospects of losing in court put me on the verge of a nervous breakdown.

It was an eerie experience for me standing in a room full of strangers were looked to cast judgement on me without actually knowing anything about me or my situation. Across room was the woman I once loved ready to fight me for custody of our child. Her presence enhanced my misgivings for the entire ordeal of going to court. Against orders from my mother, I went to court without legal representation. I can't remember my rationale for not having a lawyer but whatever the reason it was not a sensible act on my part. It was the first time in my life I surely understood what to have 'lost-love' meant.

During the early child custody proceedings, there was no doubt this would be a hard-fought court battle. People who cared deeply for me advised me not to go to court with a verbal "double barreled shotgun." They meant that I should not say what needed to be said to win no matter how bad it hurt her mother. I wanted to win and I was willing to say whatever to gain custody of Nia. A casual friend by the name of Taylor encouraged me to not hold back and tell everything that happened to the judge.

"Unload both barrels on her."

His reference to the use of a verbal shotgun made me laugh at the time. I was reluctant to do that, in a way I still loved her mother and more importantly I did not want to go that route to win.

We went to court on three more occasions during which Nia stayed with me, her mother came for her on the weekends. After the fourth court date, her mother failed to show, and the judge awarded me full custody of Nia. I never wanted things to end like they did but going on would have done more damaging to Nia than necessary. I did not gloat, jump for joy or get drunk. I cried because I felt like a failure.

There was no crystal ball to tell me where we would end up, but I had my baby. I got what I wanted, and my life would be turned upside down because of it. I was destined to get it right, in my job as a parent, as well as a teacher, despite my being a loser in love.

CHAPTER 8

For three agonizing minutes, I stood in front of my class waiting for the answer to what I thought was a straightforward question. The silence showed either my question was too difficult or my expectations for learning were misguided. I took a seat on my desk as I scanned the class for a spark in anyone's eye that would show someone had a clue.

"We've gone over the document for two days and answered questions on it for homework Friday night!" I shouted in fake exasperation. Sometimes being an actor was the best way to stoke emotions in lifeless teenagers because to show real emotions would have produced a more negative moment. The weekend of preparation for the day's lesson to assess the prior week's unit appeared to fall flat. Normally, I would have waited a short amount of time before presenting the correct answer to the class in order not to have the lesson get bogged down with the proficient students bored and the less proficient not caring. Giving the answer at that point would have maintained the all-important rhythm of the class but, since this was a review, I thought it was best to fish for my answer because everyone seemed to be at a loss. I rephrased my original question several times. The bait did not prompt the desired response from any of the students. I stood for a moment wondering if I had to check my teaching skill as if my breath were tart. This was the rare situation where each level of student struggled. In this moment, I pondered if the lack of understanding rested in my teaching, their learning or both. There was a bigger issue at hand that had an adverse effect on how I taught each lesson.

There was a constant battle raging in each class I taught centered on what was needed to pass the state test and the real history that should be taught, regardless of the demands of the state test. The question I asked wouldn't appear on the New York State Regents but it was a question that would open the student's minds to powerful facts hidden in history. Preparing the students for the uninspiring exam made teaching the nuances of history a game of picking poisons. This day I was going to make the students think on a higher level even at the expense of getting in trouble with my supervisor.

"Well, can anyone tell me what African-Slaves were freed as a result of Lincoln's 1863 Emancipation Proclamation?"

I substituted the original question with another.

"What impact did the Emancipation Proclamation have on African-Slavery during the Civil War?"

This time I was a little angry at the lack of response. The silence was such that the hum of the overhead lights became noticeable. I, then, asked the students for the second time to refer to the document I gave them in the prior lesson. Immediately pages in notebooks began to sound off as they were tossed about. One student did not bother looking at his notes because he had the answer I sought.

"Lincoln freed all the slaves."

I did not want to erode his confidence to answer questions in class therefore my response was measured for the proper effect.

"He freed all of the African Slaves in the United States?"

I countered. (The emphasis placed on the use of the term "African Slaves" was meant to remind the students that the idea of slavery began long before Africans became the modern definition of a slave.) My answer caused the students to buzz with wonder. Another student shouted out an interesting response to my opening question.

"He didn't free the slaves in the south because he did not have control of the south during the war" another student responded. I had him read an excerpt to the class to back up his claim. I was so happy at the time I extended the thought to another pivotal question.

"What section of the country was controlled by The Union?"

In unison, many of the kids shouted out the correct answer, "The North."

One student added information about the Missouri Compromise of 1819, which made my heart race with excitement. It was then a few more students began to introduce a torrent of information on the events leading up to the American Civil War but my original question was not among the responses. It was always a good policy to have the students raise their hand in class, but when there seemed to be a real interest shown in class I sometimes let the information flow loose and free. The discussion included Lincoln's "A House Divided" speech, as well as, Lincoln's pronouncements during his debates with Stephen Douglass. They had no idea that they were armed with more information needed to answer the first question posed to them. One student called Lincoln a hypocrite another claimed Lincoln was just a man of his times. I looked at my watch, which indicated it was time to begin wrapping up the lesson by trying to have the students elaborate on my initial question. Only when I went to the class map and pointed out the Four Slave States that remained loyal to the Union did my answer arrive.

"He did not have control of the South, how could he free the slaves there?" one of the students asked. The "hypocrite" notion was revisited, as was my response. I asked them to analyze Lincoln's rationale for not abolishing slavery in the north in his Emancipation Proclamation in at least two paragraphs. The mention of writing brought an immediate and overwhelmingly negative response from the class. This time my exasperation was not faked. I lived the worst moment for a comedian in my classroom.

Teaching history sometimes was a case of taking two steps forward and five steps back. In the end, the goal of educating the students would be for them to understand the importance of education. The unspoken truth was it was most important to be educated with knowledge, as much real information as possible, which would allow the students to make informed decisions. If they did their work, I believed the information I could give them would put them above the rest. My only other class fared much worse with the information I supplied. The end of the school day could not come fast enough for me, for I felt as if I was the problem and not the students.

I exited the train four stops early on 110th Street and Eighth Avenue at the northern edge of Central Park and started my trek home. I recently moved Nia and myself back with my mother. I needed the help but more importantly I needed time to think. The long walk home allowed the gradual conversion from stressed out teacher to stressed-out parent. The high blue sky made for a picture-perfect backdrop for the hard-urban landscape. My mind was focused on what I believed to be my ineptitude as a teacher at Chelsea High School. The prolonged miming of information taxed my confidence. I slowly crossed the street to 111th thus my walk home began.

By the time I reached 116th Street and Eighth Avenue I had already convinced myself that I was only a small part of the problem; that the students and their parents held a greater but equal part in the process. I stood on the corner waiting on the light to change and overlooked the former stomping grounds of some very nefarious former Harlem residents. Drug Kingpins, Leroy "Nikki" Barnes, Frank Lucas and Guy Fisher once held court very near where I stood. Thinking about those gentlemen brought to mind my students.

No one forced the drug dealers into doing wrong; for it was easier to do wrong rather than to do right. My students could have taken the time to study and prepare for class but, being unprepared, for them, was easier than putting in the hard work it would have taken to do well for that lesson. Most of the students I taught were self-motivated; they used the specter of the final marking period to get them motivated about their schoolwork. No matter how many calls I made home, the same students did the work and the same ones came to class unprepared. I continued my walk with the understanding that the administration at Chelsea felt, I was not motivating the students.

At 121st Street, I reached a familiar vacant lot that stretched to 122nd Street. Years earlier my sister Debra's son, Mario, began playing little league baseball close to the 121st street side. Oddly at the other end towards 122nd street stood a very powerful monument that had always gained my attention whenever I happened by. Someone tied two old-style telephone poles together end to end and planted it upright in the lot. If one can imagine how high a single telephone pole is, then two poles is an impressive sight. A basketball goal was tightly fastened to the very top of the end of the Pole. The words "Higher Goals" were written in bold letters. I assumed the work of art was left to inspire the residents of Harlem to set goals higher than usual. I stopped on the corner: made a pact with myself to take a picture of the goal but unfortunately, I never did. I wondered why to my knowledge no one in the media ever reported about the person who created such a unique yet powerful message. Each time I saw it I had to think about my life and the goals I set for myself.

There were many goals I set for myself, and to that point in my life, I only achieved three of them. Despite giving myself a pep talk on 121st Street I continued to feel unsure of my abilities at work. I also held the belief that I should be doing more with my life than I was at the time. Yes, I had Nia. Yes, I had a good job and a loving family but there was something missing. I assumed the missing ingredient that would make my life complete. I wrongfully assumed what was missing was money as well as the opportunity to spend the money. I resumed my walk sure that at the end I would come to a final solution. The back and forth I struggled with in adult life would not go quietly into the long goodnight.

Two blocks from my apartment building, against all facts, I had convinced myself that I should no longer remain in the teaching profession; that the kids were not picking up what I tried to teach them, as my principal suggested.

My thoughts of futility were interrupted by a glance into a bodega on the corner of 141st Street and Eighth Ave. I glanced at the store out of habit and came upon the smile of a pretty young girl. Her complexion was dark, and she had to be in her early twenties and she had no business smiling at my old ass. I was nice looking, but there were more important things on my mind than a twinkle in a young girl's eyes. As I turned away to continue my walk home the young girl exited the store and called out my last name, which stopped me in my tracks.

"Mr. Lawson, I thought that was you."

She said with a smile on her face. My thoughts changed from a young girl trying to flirt with me to a former student trying to reconnect with her recent past. She walked up to me and gave me a huge hug when she spoke words that were like manna for my soul.

"I want to thank you Mr. Lawson," she said as she released her hold upon me.

"Thank me for what?"

I tried my best to remember her name and the school where I taught her.

"You made class interesting and you kept me in school."

Her answer to my internal questioning lifted my spirits higher than any goal I had set for myself. Sticking to form, I deflected all praises and placed them onto her deeds.

"You did all the work. All I did was facilitate," I answered as I tried my best to recall her name without making it obvious. She told me that she worked in the dialysis center a few doors down from where we stood. Through conversation, I learned that I taught her at JHS 57 in Bedford-Stuyvesant (Bed-Stuy) Brooklyn, as well as her name which faded from memory like so many names of former students. After a polite conversation about the old days and people at the Brooklyn Junior High School, as we parted ways, I wondered how many other students held a positive opinion of my teaching skills. My inner voice answered my thought.

"It did not matter as much what others thought of me more than what I thought of myself."

I entered after I stopped to greet many of the people, sitting in front of the building, by name. Once inside I began to sweat from the immense heat in the lobby of the building. It was not hot outside, but the lobby was at its normal temperature. After waiting an eternity with other residents for the elevator, I decided to run the ten fights up the stairs rather than pile onto a crowded elevator or wait in the hot lobby for the next car to arrive. I hadn't taken my first step up the stairs when Juicy exited the stairwell and informed me that my mother had just taken Nia upstairs and Nia was acting out with her grandmother. I thanked her and bounded the stairs to the tenth floor as I had done all through high school.

I told my mother the story about my former student after I was able to catch my breath. My mind may have thought that I was 18 again but the burning in my legs told my real age. My mother listened to my story and she dispensed well thought out advice.

"You keep teaching, and someone will learn."

I kissed her all over her forehead, which made her laugh.

"It will take time with Nia and it will take time for those kids to learn but you keep teaching and don't let anyone establish your worth as a teacher to the world" she said as she finally stopped her laughing. As I walked to my room where I was sure Nia was playing music on my CD player, my thoughts were on how far Nia had progressed and how much more I had to achieve as a teacher.

Silence Is Not Always Golden

There is something I have always found adorable in the inability of a young child to express their thoughts in a clear and succinct manner. The honest way they attempt to finish their thought always brings a smile to my face because in their struggle to lay out their thoughts learning is taking place. For whatever reason the child will get stuck on a word or phrase that hijacks the conversation. They stumble around for a moment like a prize fighter who has stepped into the ring one to many times in an attempt to rescue their fleeting thought.

Usually, the child gives up trying to explain and goes off to play. The innocent way a young child tries to communicate lasts only a brief period. Soon the child develops enough skills to hold an uninterrupted conversation that may come at the most inconvenient time for the parent. Nia never provided me with that opportunity; sounds did not count as words and parroting a conversation does not show understanding.

Whenever I hear a parent complain that their child needs to shut up and be quiet, I pray for their problem. It is my assertion that parents sometimes do not have the tools to answer a tough question presented by their child. Other times to answer their inquisitive offspring would lead to a prolonged session that the parent did not want to take place on topics that should not be discussed outside the home. A child that is always told to "Be quiet" by their parent has been done a disservice, because it could discourage future communication or worse stymie a child's inquisitiveness.

There were many aspects of raising Nia alone I did foresee. One was the long periods of time in a day I would go without having a meaningful conversation with another person. Often the first lengthy conversation of the day would take place with Nia's bus driver or matron. The conversation would more or less be the same each day. The last guaranteed conversation would take place when I picked Nia up off the bus at the end of the school day. I am a very talkative person and to go hours in the day without a chance someone would talk back to me was a difficult adjustment for me to make. Many days I longed to have a conversation of longer than a few sentences that would make my confined world part of the broader universe. When I did receive a reprieve from the silence usually via the phone, it would be brief because I had to tend to my lesson plans or take care of Nia's needs. Nia was the only person I could talk to and whether she understood me or not, she was going to hear my voice.

From the time Nia was young I talked with her as if she could talk back to me. If my holding a one-way conversation with my baby helped her I am not sure, but it made me feel connected to a larger world. To this day hearing a parent tell a child they talk too much makes me close my eyes and wish. From the time Nia was young, I spoke to her as if she could respond to me.

CHAPTER 9

My encounter with my former student gave me a much-needed boost of confidence. Talking to her gave hope that maybe I had reached more students than just her including my current students. My mother's words also reinforced my belief that what I was doing with Nia would pay dividends one day.

I went about the task of teaching Nia as if she were like any other kid her age. Goals were set by me for Nia I thought were achievable and would help her later in life. I had to make sure she would be able to take care of her own basic needs. The less I did for her, the less dependent she would be on me. Patience was needed in abundance on my part, because it would take me four years to teach her to put on her socks and shoes without help. Just like my students, I could not give up; I had to do my best. Two hours after I arrived home from work I was back out in the street on my way to the place where I could recharge my mental batteries and escape. My mother did not mind watching Nia for a few hours because as she said I needed to hang out with thirty somethings like myself instead of Nia. The idea of going one day without taking Nia to the park was a good change of routine.

I exited the elevator into the lobby of the building cursing my decision of taking the slow elevator rather than the stairs. I stepped over the garbage that littered the floor of the elevator and into the perennially hot lobby and ran into someone I had not seen in a very long time. His shabby attire and troubled look on his face was a far cry from the young man who used to garner attention. K.J. was as smooth as any brother that lived in 310. His thick curly hair, as well as his swagger, made him a favorite of many girls in the building and the neighborhood. When he moved around there were always lusty female

73

eyes upon him. For all his good looks and charm, K.J. was a flawed individual that allowed him to fall to the streets. He began a long spiral downward, which ended with him being hooked on drugs. Every time he saw me he knew he could ask for money and I would give him a few dollars. With the money always came a plea from me to turn his life around. K.J. was polite in his response but it did not appear to me that he would ever turn his life around.

"Yo' Dee"

He said. He never called me by my entire name just Dee.

"I want to…"

Immediately I got a defensive look on my face. I just knew he was about to ask me for money. I told him the last time would be the last time if he did not clean up his act. K.J. saw my reaction and addressed it in a voice that made me feel embarrassed for thinking what I did.

"Dee, I don't want nothing from you. I wanted to give you this."

He held out his hand in it was a green colored pocket Bible.

"I wanted to thank you for looking out for me" he said as he handed it to me.

I had no choice but to accept it because to do otherwise would be a sign of disrespect to him and the book. I placed the gift in my pocket and made my way out of the door but not without, once again, encouraging him to clean up his life. The next two times I would see K.J. he looked as if he had started up the long stairway to a better life, but addiction is a hard thing to break. I exited the building with thoughts of how his life had been altered by drugs.

Heading to my old block meant that I would have to cross several unofficial cultural border lines in upper Manhattan. I would move from Central Harlem, to Hamilton Heights then to Washington Heights. Two decades earlier they were all considered part of the greater Harlem but change is the only constant in life.

I had to walk up a steep incline that was 145th Street west to Broadway. My walk took me past the brownstone where Antarctic explorer Matthew Henson once lived. Harlem is a history buffs dream. Near Convent Avenue I had to stop to take a breather and once more I ran into a former student. This encounter was a melancholy one.

Arnold Douglass was a student at I.S. 136 when I was a second-year teacher there. I was not fully indoctrinated to my life as a schoolteacher, but I should have known better. Every kid deserves the full attention of adults that teach them, but he was the only student I gave up on. I felt there was something about him that suggested that no matter how hard I tried, he would have little success in school. At the end of the school year, Paul's mother approached me as I escorted my class on a field trip. She looked at me dead in my face and advocated for her son. "You gave up on my child didn't you?" I was stunned. I don't remember my response but his mother knew I had regarded her child as a useless human. The idea that I felt that way and acted on it is the blackest mark on me as a black man. Arnold was about over six foot tall and lanky as a youth. As a man in his mid-twenties, Arnold was wafer thin. He was dark skinned, but his unkempt appearance made him look even darker. His eyes were glossy, and it was plain to see he was high on something. I caught his eye and he stopped.

"Hey, You, what's up Lawson?" he said as he extended his hand to me. I grasp his hand but I looked hard at his thumb on his right hand. His thumb was stained yellow from holding a joint between his fingers as he puffed his life away.

"I am chillin' but, you have to stay up Paul" I said as I tightened my handshake to accentuate my statement. I took a long look at his thumbs for more evidence to prove my suspicions.

"I'm chillin',"

He said with a smile which showed me he knew what I was talking about. He continued on his way and me on mine. I stopped to look back at Paul. We would meet that way many times over the years and each time, he was no better. I shook my head out of guilt and continued on my way.

I reached Broadway and turned north to stroll by the Nova Theater, which once was called the Tapia when I was a pre-teen. We neighborhood kids would flock to the sticky-floored theater to see the latest Kung Fu picture or 'Blaxploitation' movie. Going to that theater each weekend taught me three great lessons. I learned the meaning of the word frugal: when I had to politic with my father to get enough money to get into the movies, buy popcorn and a soda. I came to understand that racial issues are open ended propositions and I learned that I wanted to marry a foxy, Coffey complexioned woman like Pamela Grier. How parents allowed their kids to walk to the theater and watch rated R movies I never would know, but I am glad they did.

One block north of the Nova on the Uptown side of the avenue once stood the famous *Broadway International Disco*. Gone was the original marquee replaced by the 99 Cent Store that took over the building. In front of the venue, I was shoved aside by the bodyguards of five boys from Boston who were set to perform on stage ahead of their first album release in 1984. I was angered to the point that I did not stay to see them go on stage. In retrospect I missed out on a historical moment.

Further up the avenue, on the same side of Broadway International stood another venue that shaped my early childhood. *The Oasis* was like the Ponderosa in that they both had the notorious reputation. I never ventured inside The *Oasis,* but I took the hearsay about what went on inside as fact. Seeing the red and white stripe awning served as a symbol of the fight against right and wrong. I surfaced from my thoughts on the corner of 150th Street and Broadway to wait for several cars to drive by. On that same block once lived LL Cool Jay's first D.J, the author of *Invisible Man* and the Apollo's dancing legend. I had met the D.J. through his brother and I appreciated his greatness.

The approach of a sexy Dominican honey ended the nostalgia and put my mind to something else. She noticed me looking at her, I smiled at her and she smiled back but did not stop. A smile from a woman was all I could handle at the time; besides she was not as fine as the women I fell in love with in the movies. I took a good look at her then turned toward my destination, the corner of 151st Street and Broadway and I had to rub my eyes wondering if I had in fact gone time traveling.

I could see four old friends standing on the corner. Chiba, Patch, Rock, and Kevin stood in the very same location years ago. The corner served as a forum for us, the kids on the block. We met on the corner before we went to school or when we left the block. From morning to night, we played either Chinese handball or crate basketball there until the store owner would chase us away. Years later, large amounts of drugs were bought and sold on our beloved corner which ended it as a place to hang out.

It was on that corner I lost what was left of my naivety when I just missed seeing a double homicide as I went to the corner store to purchase a Suzy Q and Onion Garlic Potato Chips. I would also stand on the corner waiting for my father to come home from work on Fridays.

The best time spent on the corner was spent cracking jokes on each other so, that day, as soon as I was close enough to them, jokes were hurled at me, with love. The five of us spent more than [a] half an hour rehashing jokes that never seemed to get old. We made fun of Sonny's "Widows Peak" as well as his prolific use of the word "Fuck" in his spoken language. He was the first black person I knew that studied Kung Fu and his nickname, came from his favorite martial arts actor, Sonny Chiba. Chiba was not one to cross and had some epic fights on the Avenue growing up. Once we finished "snapping" on Chiba, it was Kevin's turn to be roasted.

He was reminded how his late girlfriend would interrupt whatever we were doing to have him run errands with her. There were many times we could not finish a 'skellies' or stickball game because Kevin was summoned by his girlfriend. We laughed at how Rock's mother and cousin had him on lockdown. He could not do anything, but he always seemed to be with us anyway. Eventually, Rock's mother and cousin moved him to Connecticut to keep him out of trouble and away from us. They did a good job because Rock became a foreman on major construction sites. Between the snaps, we talked about how Rock, Kevin and another crew member, Danny were good neighborhood M.C.'s who could have been great if they put the time into the craft. Since I could not rap, I held out hope of being their EC, equipment carrier. I laughed to erase the sight of Chiba standing over Danny's hospital bed while the latter was on life support, with tubes extending from his mouth and nose. His head was crushed from making contact with the subway support columns after jumping off a moving subway car. The only time I ever saw Sonny shed tears was at Danny's bedside.

They made fun of my unofficial nickname of L.L. and how I got it. Kevin reminded everyone how I broke my arm by riding down the hill in a shopping cart. Sonny retold the story of how I got beat under a car by the Kruger sisters. (It was a long time before I would ever call a girl out her name.) Rock told how I used to play with ants. The laughter turned to Patch, who was the last to be snapped upon.

The jokes on Patch had to be well conceived because he was very good at comebacks. I know he would not believe this but, I have the utmost respect for Patch. Patch experienced many ups and downs in his life but in the end, he managed to stay up and kicking. Even a horrific accident that caused great harm to his body could not keep him down for long. He did the best with his situation, which left me no room to complain about my troubles. Through it all, Patch kept his sense of humor and his ability to look at the world through rose-colored glasses. There was no doubt had our situations been switched, I would not have been standing on the corner telling jokes.

After an entirety of ruminating, we decided to leave the corner due to the annoying glares of the corner boys. The corner was still considered "hot" and it was a matter time someone considered grown men laughing on a known drug corner a threat and they had us against the wall. One by one we reverted back to our present lives leaving the past until the next time we got together.

Sonny had to get home before his wife came looking for him, therefore, his exit was swift. Patch was on his way to his Aunt's house on The Lower East Side of Manhattan before he boarded the bus back to his home in Georgia the next day. Rock had a long drive to his home in Connecticut. He had to be to work at 5 Am and traffic could have him on the road too long. Their departure left Kevin and me alone for the moment. He needed to get something from his apartment, therefore, we left the corner.

I followed Kevin to his house. Kevin was the first cousin of another good friend Cleveland, which made him a brother from another mother and father. As we walked down the very hill that we ran up and down, day and night, long ago, he stopped to talk to a host of people who approached him. He was a popular longtime resident of the block, with a magnetic personality and a great laugh that had not changed from the time we were teenagers.

Kevin was a superior athlete. In baseball, he was a five-tool player before the word was used to identify outstanding baseball talent. When he was not throwing a baseball a mile, his cannon of a right arm tossed a football the distance of three sewers. Only Sonny and Cleveland could match his skill in baseball and only Dynamite, from 152nd Street could match his arm in football. Newton could run faster, leaving Kevin a close second. I spent my entire teenaged years trying to measure up to all the boys I called friend; especially Kevin. He bested me in athletic ability in addition to school. We both attended Charles Evans Hughes High School as freshmen where he received a grade of 95 in Algebra and I managed a paltry grade of 45. Irony would have me teach in the same building under a different name.

When I transferred from Hughes to John F. Kennedy High School to play football as a motivator to graduation, I told Kevin he should join me. I was able to make the football team but I sucked and knew with his skills Kevin would be a starter in no time. He declined, choosing instead to stay on the block, he needed to make money to support his children thus, began his odyssey.

Each time I returned from college, one of my first stops was to head up the hill to check him out and make sure he was good. Sitting in his bedroom, years later, on his rare day off, right in the middle of the conversation about old friends including Saladin Keith, Kevin made a comment that caught me by surprise.

"I don't know how you do it, Dee. If any of my children were special needs I couldn't handle it,"

He mentioned as he got off his bed and walked over to toss his pack of cigarettes onto the nearby dresser before he continued his thoughts.

"I don't know how her mother…"

He soberly noted. He lost his train of thought as he spotted the job idea he'd lost for a month. I had never heard him speak about Nia that way and there was no denying the statement had been on his mind for some time. My heart sank a bit hearing this from the guy who could carry heavy construction materials around as if it were pillows. I marveled at the strength I doubted I owned. I did not know what to say so my standard line was readily available for use.

"If you were in my shoes, I know you could do a good job."

He gave me a confused look then answered in kind.

"No, I could not!"

I looked at him with one eyebrow raised, because what he'd done was much more difficult than being Nia's father. He helped to raise kids before he was in tenth grade. I could not imagine being in his shoes for more than a minute and not losing my mind. We each sat in awe of the accomplishments of the other, neglecting to acknowledge what we have done in our own right. The conversation about *Life* ended. A long uncomfortable pause served as a buffer for our conversation about our favorite sports teams. My talk with Kevin that day made me feel good that I did not walk into the K-Building when I presumed I could not go on any further. Yes, I was in my early thirties, but I spent most of that decade looking at my life with Nia and nothing much else. I did not see all I had done for my daughter and how others may not be able to do what I had and will do for Nia. At times I would be down on myself believing I could not do any more, only to summon the strength to go on.

As a teenager, I compared myself to all my friends and it was always easy to say how I was not confident in all endeavors like Ennis, philosophical like Levine or could sing with the likes of Ferguson or Mitchell. I was unable to match them in any way, but had I had my conversation with Kevin back then I would have understood I could only be me.

I had Nia and I did not have to compare my life to anyone else, for I was another unique entity God placed on this earth. People were watching me, some in awe, of how a man raised his Special Needs Child essentially alone. I could never give up on myself because there were many people who wanted me to succeed.

CHAPTER 10

Being a father and a teacher gave me the ability to have a unique perspective on each vocation. One job gave me insight into the other which allowed me to become better at both. Nia gave me patience which was transferred to my students who were sometimes unwilling or unable to get the correct answer on the second or third try. I was thrown a curve at work when I was given two Special Education Global History classes. A Special Education License was required to teach Special Education Students in those days. In the 1990's Principals found ways around the license issue, there was more a need to educate that population and the rules were often broken. I didn't have a license but I was a warm body and the temperament not to be run out of the class in defeat. I was forced to teach the classes and I knew it was just another sign that my time was nearly up.

My first teaching permanent assignment ever was this same type of student body at I.S. 136. It was hell for me. For six months, I dealt with the kids no other teacher in the 7th grade wanted to in their class: which taught me to avoid working with difficult students if at all possible. The students cursed each other as well as cursed me. One female would bite her tongue and call attention to the blood dripping from the self-inflicted wound. Working at I.S. 136 was an 'over-the-top' experience for any teacher, let alone a first-year teacher: which made the students at Chelsea High School easier, but they proved to be a challenge.

Early on I learned that teaching content was not as important as improving social and life skills for lower performing students. I had to relate the content to things relevant to their lives. The lessons dealing with government events such as revolutions had to be related to family situations. Basic understanding of the topic was the main goal for me. I was a bricklayer and had to build a strong foundation for each student in hopes that in the end, they would be able to use their newfound skills to learn and interpret things on their own. Sometimes just getting the *Do-Now* completed was the entire lesson. Sometimes someone made an inappropriate comment that needed to be addressed.

When behavior was an issue there was only Dean Stone to call, because most of the kids in this group were in his English classes. The response to bad behavior, cursing in the class, or aggressive actions had to be measured because each student had an Individual Education Plan or IEP. The IEP were the goals for each student set by parent and teacher. If the IEP indicated that the child had a propensity to curse, or be violent when threatened, then those behaviors had to be excused, to a point. Calling home or intervention took precedence over suspension.

During one class a student stood up and began to speak in a sexual manner to another student in the class. He then began to act out what he allegedly did to a girl the prior night. I was not happy when he returned to class with only a plea by Dean Stone for him to act appropriately in class; the student's IEP indicated his behaviors were part of his disability. My time in that class made me think about Nia and what would be included in her IEP.

Parent Teacher Night, took on a new meaning for me as I advocated for Nia. I asked about her behavior as well as how she got along with the staff. I did not have to worry about Nia cursing out the staff or her classmates, or so I thought because her limited speech prevented such outbreaks. I was always told at a parent-teacher meeting she was a handful but no major problem. Nia was not a threat to hurt others, which was not like some of the students at Chelsea.

Overall it was not a very bad school, but like anywhere with a large group of teenagers' small events can turn into physical confrontations. I can remember during a conversation I had with Boys' Basketball Head Coach Hernandez about the upcoming season and my role as both the Head Coach of the Boy's Junior Varsity team and assistant on the Varsity team when a call came over the radio about a fight outside in the park. I left Coach Hernandez and dashed out of the building to the location of the fight outside of the park that was Next to the school. I arrived just in time to be instructed by Dean Stone and Sargent Coats to take one of the girls inside the building and have her write a statement.

The student I escorted inside the building was known well by me. She lived close to me and sometimes we rode the same train to Chelsea. She was a tough Harlem girl who would never bother anyone but if they bothered her she would forget her manners in a hurry. As I walked her back to the building I did something that I never did again before or after; I asked the young lady a question.

If a student were caught with a weapon the student would be Superintendent Suspended for up to one year. I once was involved in a case where a freshman student was kicked out of the school because his brother wore his jacket to work at the local supermarket. The brother left a box cutter in the jacket and the boy pleaded with us that it was not his. His pleas didn't prevent his suspension, but I asked the hearing officer for 15 days, the least suspension time and for the boy to be returned to the school. The hearing officer agreed with the recommendation of the school but in the end, the student never returned.

Another incident had me come upon a student who dropped his seven-inch knife at my feet in the middle of the crowded hallway. I had no ill feelings about sending that student packing. There were other students I was instructed to suspend by the Administration some of which had better results in the class after being placed in another school. I am not sure if subconsciously these things were on my mind when I asked my question.

"Do you have anything on you, you should not have?"

I asked without thinking of the consequences. She pulled a broken car antenna from out of her bag and handed it to me.

She confessed before she continued.

"She has been bothering me for a long time. Today I was going to fuck her up."

The young girl confessed without any emotion. I took the antenna from her and placed it in my jacket as I had the young girl write a statement. I left her just for a moment to get the statement form and was sidetracked for the next hour. By the time I returned to the office and the student the conflict had been mediated and both girls shook hands. I was the last to leave the room and no one said anything about the antenna and neither did I. It was left in the garbage can in the office for the custodian to dispose of. The custodian at Chelsea also played a pivotal role in my best detective work.

After dismissal one day, while I was performing vertical sweeps on the building I ran into my good friend as he cleaned the stairwell. He was one of the hardest working men I knew because this was his second job of the day. The first was a cook in the kitchen from morning until afternoon. He also helped buy Boys' Varsity and Junior Varsity Basketball badly needed uniforms. When I could not find Coach Hernandez, I picked his brain for his knowledge of basketball.

"Lawson man, if I find the kid who has been pissing in this stairwell I might lose my job" he said in frustration. What upset the man was that he cleaned up urine in the stairwell more than he should. I promised to find the culprit and the mission began. Each day after dismissal I went to the stairwell to search for the student, but I came up empty. The culprit continued to empty his bladder without being caught. There were days when I forgot to check but my friend did not forget his anger.

"You need to find him, Lawson" he warned once again. I took his warning seriously. As I sat on the stairwell right after dismissal with my radio turned down I watched from above as someone entered the stairwell and walked right over to the spot where the culprit had been urinating. I waited as a herd a zipper open and pants come down. A called out to the person I walked down the stairs to confront the individual. The culprit was a boy as the custodian and I suspected. The call I placed to the home of the student left me shaking my head. His mother informed me that her son was intimidated by boys in the bathroom and he chose to urinate in the staircase rather than inform the school. I could not believe the Presidential like defense of her child.

"There are other bathrooms to use in the school, however you nor you son expressed his fears to any of the 60 adults in the building."

My retort went unanswered. She was full of crap and she knew there was no real defense for her son's pissing in the staircase every day. The boy was suspended for three days and for once I felt the suspension should have been longer.

My time at Chelsea came to an end the following year when Mr. Jenson handed me my "Excess Papers." I left the building headed for a new school amongst tearful goodbyes from the students and staff.

CHAPTER 11

"When one door closes…" begins the most often Christian used phrases used today. The very end of that phrase tells of a new beginning better than the door that closed. The door that closed saw Nia's mother leave our lives; the door that opened was the future with my child. As mentioned earlier, I had a failed marriage that eventually led me back to my parent's apartment after my father's death. Going back home gave me the chance to refocus my attention back to my duties as a parent as well as help with raising Nia.

At the point in time that I moved back home my spirits were very low, but I had to persevere and excel. The everyday needs of taking care of Nia did not diminish with my moving in with my mother. My state of mind changed from *'if'* I could get things done, to *'How'* do I get things done. The change might seem incremental to a linguist but to a psychologist, the change could be monumental.

Despite her age, she continued to have a tendency to put objects into her mouth. Gone were the metal hangers that could damage her teeth and cut up her mouth replaced with a spoon that could knock out her teeth possibly choking her. Nia was able to take a bath with limited assistance from me and she was able to put on her favorite camisole to walk around the apartment. She learned to say and write her first name as well. With all the change happening one thing stayed the same.

The one constant was a two-time loser in life just like the one Theodore Pendergrass sang about in his "Love T.K.O." The idea of failing twice left a hole in my heart. The whole in my heart could not be filled by natural means, therefore, I needed my friends and my family more than ever.

I had no brothers, but I consider several men to be my brothers. They gave me the spirit I needed not to look back only forward, I had Bryant Garfield Smith.

Bryant and I met in college at Grambling State University in Louisiana in 1985 and became fast friends. At Grambling, Bryant did not go by his birth name he went by his unique nickname. Bryant was a large man and once wore a black and yellow sweater during his rap performance during a campus talent show. Someone in the audience shouted out that he looked like a rather large Killer Bee, the name stuck and from that point on Bryant was known as Killer Bee, but he should have been called a Renaissance man.

As noted Killer could rap, he may have beaten the famous West Coast Rapper WD-80 during the talent show where he gained his nickname. He could sing, dance, play three musical instruments, DJ and was a mathematical genius. The college administration asked him to tutor several NFL bound athletes. Killer was a calm but firm fellow and could recite the Bible back and forth. We became such good friends that he sang at my father's funeral and two days later I spoke at his father's funeral. Bryant helped to keep me in college and he dispensed sound financial advice that I wished I had followed. He was disgusted with me for fighting with Nia's mother yet he was concerned when I told him I would seek custody of Nia. He always had my back and I would one day have to speak on the topic in public.

"How is the move back to your mother's house going?" Killer asked over the phone. His voice was Barry White-ish and he often cleared his throat after he made a strong point.

"I have adjusted well and to my surprise, Nia has too."

I responded as I looked out of the window at the busy street below. My thoughts were focused on the reason for my moving back home. I was not sure how Killer would react therefore looking out of the window down on *Bradhurst* was a way to relax my thoughts. Killer didn't get into them he just turned his attention to Nia.

"How are you going to get her to school? How are you going to manage financially? What kind of money are you going to pay your mother for rent?"

He asked with rapid succession. I had not thought about these questions and I could count on him to ask questions that made me think in-depth. Being that Nia was a Special Education Student she would be bussed to school. I was under the impression a simple phone call would change her pick-up and drop off location. Moving back home would begin to save me money in the long run because I would only pay half of what I paid at my former home. Once Killer received his answers he began to ask questions: better yet made suggestions I had not contemplated on my own. He wanted to know if I was ready to take on the job of raising Nia for the rest of her life.

"I have no choice. I was granted custody I can't turn back now!"

I responded. There was no way I wanted to think that far ahead but Killer was a businessman too and he always had to think about contingency plans. It was Killer's way of making me prepare myself for the task ahead. A moment of silence allowed me to change the subject onto one that did not make me feel the least bit uncomfortable. The subject turned to one of the many things we had in common, Grambling State University.

One of the ways I burned off my frustration was to represent Grambling at Historically Black College Fairs around New York City. We would spend our Saturdays pitching the virtues of a Grambling Education and telling stories about our experiences there. Sometimes McDowell, Haywood, and Dubois all of whom attended Grambling, joined Killer and I in representing Grambling at area college fairs. On this day, I would head to a college fair alone and I had to get ready. Without much fanfare Killer and I ended our conversation and I moved to get ready for my long day solo act. I put on my black jeans with black dress shoes and my gold colored Grambling sweatshirt and walked out my room heading for the living room.

The room I slept in once belonged to my big sister Jacqueline. She moved out and left the dark purple rug accented by the light purple paint on the walls. I vowed to change the rug and the paint, but painting would have to wait. I had other things more important than painting and removing paint. Upon leaving the room I looked into the open door of my old bedroom, which belonged to Nia. As I peered into the room it was clear we had not made ourselves at home.

Prior to our moving back home the room had been used by my mother as a storage room. Aside from the clothes and boxes stacked in the room, there was a hospital bed that was intended for my one-of-a-kind uncle Alfred. He was set to live with my mother, but he lost his fight with diabetes. There was much work to be done in order to make her room livable. In the meantime, Nia would sleep with her grandmother until I got around to cleaning the room.

I made a sharp right turn and headed up the hall past the two bathrooms towards the living room of the three-bedroom apartment. The closer I was to the living room the more a favorite smile took hold of my senses. Saturday pancakes and bacon were the welcome I had hoped I would receive but was dampened by the look on my mother's face.

Through the hutch, I could see her face and there was something troubling her. As a child, I had gotten into enough trouble to know when she was upset and like most kids, I had to ask to make sure she was not angry with me.

"What's the matter, mother?"

I asked as I took a seat at the dining room table, which was directly underneath the hutch. She looked over her glasses as she responded to my query.

"You have to do something with that girl. She has been up since 6 AM."

Nia discovered that our local cable station recently programmed twenty-four hours of children's shows and her favorite show of that time *Barney* came on at that ungodly hour. My fear was that Nia, if left unchecked, might walk out the door or do something to harm herself. Her irregular sleep pattern was the result of several factors including discovering *Barney*.

If she did not have enough to eat at night she could awake around 4 AM looking for something to eat. This would last for several years. If she slept too long during a nap she could stay up late, which would throw her sleep off the next day. All this could be overridden by her not being in the bed by 8PM. I noticed that on good days Nia would begin to fall asleep 7 PM. If I were out of the house with her and allowed her to fall asleep, then somewhere getting her undressed Nia would awake and have energy enough to stay awake until 2 AM. Her erratic sleep caused me a great deal of stress because I could not find anyone who wanted to watch her overnight if there would ever be an overnight. Countless times I wrestled with the one issue I had avoided for a very long time. I looked up at my mother and finally came to the end of the avoidance issue.

"Monday, I will look into getting her off her current medication. I hate doing it but her lack of sleep is not just affecting me."

I spoke with a heavy heart because there was no longer a need to pretend that I could handle Nia without any external help. My mother looked through the hutch at my face and she must have recognized defeat register on it. As most mothers tend to do she wanted to lift my spirits and she sought to do this is two ways.

"You can try the medication and if you don't like the results you can always stop using it."

She stopped what she was doing in the kitchen to give me her full attention. These were the same things my father said, I did not follow. Hearing it again from my mother this time was proof that my parents were correct and failure to act on my part could be a terrible choice. I remember looking down at the green linoleum patterned floor of the kitchen as I searched for the courage to answer my mother's suggestion. There was no clear reason why going on the same way with Nia would produce a different result. I looked up and gave my mother my reluctant answer. She made me give my response again, I guess to make sure I could not back down: then she went about her task of completing cooking.

The idea did lift my spirits for I forgot nothing has to last forever. What lifted my spirits even higher was the thought of my mother fixing me pancakes and bacon for breakfast. It was not simply the food that lifted me it was the notion that for the first time in eight years I found a place of peace. My sense of peace brought about an important question of where was Nia.

"She was in my bed the last time I saw her" my mother said. I could tell from the empty plate that Nia had already eaten her breakfast and her whereabouts was a source of interest to me. I playfully called out her name to which she responded in laughter. I got up from the table to walk over to the doorway of my mother's bedroom. From there I could see Nia was buried under the covers of the bed. She continued to giggle which warmed my heart. Nia at four years of age and her speech was still limited, however, her laughter was a great substitute for words.

"Nia, where are you?" I sang out to her as I moved closer and closer to the bed. In the back of my mind I hoped she would one day respond with "Here I am," but until that day her laughter would suffice. I called out her name several more times before I leaped onto the bed beside her. Nia popped her head out from under the covers then covered herself up once again. Her laughter became more intense and I called her name and tickled her at the same time. I enjoyed the light moment for they had been far and between. The more she laughed the more I saw her mother in Nia. I wanted more from life but all I had was what was in front of me and if happiness was to come, appreciation would have to be a major part of my mindset.

MEDICATION

To medicate or not to medicate is the question many parents face whether their children are diagnosed with an ailment be it mental or physical. For me, I had to wrestle with that issue for years before I relented. There was something about giving my child medication that made me feel uncomfortable.

The first issue I had with medicating Nia was the vast array of drugs available on the market. Secondly, it was important to pinpoint the behaviors that needed to end. Nia was hyperactive and very impulsive as well as sleep deprived. I had to find a medication that would solve those issues and mitigate any side effects. The potential of side effects made my choice even more difficult.

When Nia was a toddler, there were medications that were widely prescribed one of which was called Ritalin. My experience with the drug was second hand but swayed my thoughts. There was a student at Chelsea High School that was on Ritalin. When he did not take his medication, he was hyper, and his behavior was unpredictable. The staff, including myself would chase him around the building to force him to the nurse's office to take his dosage. When he did take his medication, he appeared to be someone else. Experiencing his highs and lows made taking that particular drug not worth the trouble. I was against the drug that before the psychiatrist finished his recommendation of Ritalin I answered in the negative. The psychiatrist then suggested another drug, the name I can no longer recall but I wanted to be a man of my word and give medication a try.

My first choice of drugs for Nia left me unsatisfied because she lost her appetite and still did not sleep. Very importantly, I expressed my reasons for my displeasure with the medication to her psychiatrist and together we searched for another drug called Strattera. This drug did what I needed it to do to make our lives easier.

Nia's long nights were a thing of the past and most of her impulsive behaviors disappeared. She became less frenetic in her actions almost a docile child. She no longer stood in front of the television to block its view, which would make anyone in the apartment shout her name to her delight. Nia became more manageable and much more predictable in her behavior. Despite my joy of getting more sleep at night, there were some side effects that took away from the benefits of using Strattera.

I administered the Strattera daily as directed, the template of missing one dose was firmly ingrained in my mind. Giving Nia her medication added to my list of jobs I needed to do for Nia like giving her a bath or brushing her teeth. I was not upset with the added duties because the positive impact was almost immediate. The results made me happy but with everything there is always a flipside.

Along with the good comes the bad, and with the longer sleep came some undesirable trade-off. Since I had to give Nia her medication in the morning Nia often went to school very lethargic. I did not inform her school that she was on medication because I wanted them to have an unbiased opinion of my child. If the school would have known the school would have made it difficult for me keep control over Nia. Had Nia's school known she was on medication there could have been pressure on me to keep Nia on a specific medication or that I keep her medicated. These were my fears even if they sound silly, but I had to call the same student's parent on more than one occasion. Insisting the school environment was better when he was on his medication. We could not force her but we could be a pain in her neck if she didn't comply. I did not want that for my child or for me because she was young with many years of schooling ahead of her.

Nia's behavior was such that I would get calls about her disrobing in class during her temper tantrums and dancing like Beyoncé on the lunchroom tables. If she was doing that and the school knew she was on meds they could have begun the process of kicking her out the school. Nia lost much of her appetite when she was on Strattera. She was a picky eater, to begin with but what she liked Nia ate. It troubled me to see her pass up meal after meal. Her lack of an appetite and her glassy-eyed look even caught the attention of my cousin's Chanequa and Zanetta who shared their thoughts with me on the subject of medication. Chanequa complained during one family function. Zanetta chimed in on Nia's energy level while on the mediation.

"I Don't like Nia like this she ain't eating enough food" she pronounced. When others in my family expressed the same reservations about Nia I had to take another look at the risks. I adjusted the dosage amount I gave her each day, half a pill instead of a whole pill. I did this on my own without consulting the psychiatrist. The change made her less lethargic but the effects of the medication were compromised.

"I am used to the active Nia, not the present one who looks like a zombie!" she announced. I was surprised by Zanetta's reaction because she was the recipient of much of Nia's antics.

Nia's hyperactive nature was difficult at times to handle but the alternative of her being a zombie was too high a price for me. Some parents may have enjoyed a quiet child who slept most of the day and made very little noise, but for me, I did not like seeing my child as another person, one that was not growing as an individual but stagnate and dull. I made the choice to medicate Nia and I also made the choice to change her dosage. I felt the power should rest in my hands and not the hands of someone who does not live with my child.

The main point of placing your child on medication is sticking with it. There is no point in starting your child on medication if you are not going to give it to them as directed. It does a child more harm than good to alter the plan. I was told that more than once and eventually I did take her off medication. I did this on the advice of the psychiatrist when I informed him of what the changes made to Nia's dosage. It was then I learned from the psychiatrist that sometimes the patients outgrow the medication.

My decision to medicate Nia was tough for me and the one to alter it was equally tough, but each served their purpose. Nia had changed for the better due to medication but the idea that all the medications could harm her liver made it much easier to halt medication. The essence of Nia was still alive and well without the medication: but along with coming to grips with her needs, I had to learn the remedy for my problems.

Parents of Special Needs kids might look like super beings because they do a job not many would want to do for longer than a day. What appears to be hard as stone could actually be brittle just under the surface, therefore, look out for the *parent*. Supply them with all the assistance possible because they may feel as I did about medication on other matters of their child. It took time to listen to those who love me, and when I did my life and the life of my child improved, marginally.

CHAPTER 12

My responsibilities as Nia's father played havoc with my once full social calendar. In place of the romantic nights out with a sexy lady or chillin' with the fellas, were quickly replaced with taking care of Nia and grading papers Monday through Friday. The weekend did not become my days of rest because I needed to get out of the apartment.

Weekend mornings I would take Nia to one of the parks in the neighborhood as a way of getting her day started. We would arrive before most of the neighborhood kids were there to avoid roughhousing and access to the equipment. She would enjoy the sliding board and if hot enough she would dip her feet in the sprinklers, afterward we were on the subway for parts unknown. Our routine went on for years without much deviation. As my days became predictable I was sure I was the only person on earth that was enjoying all life had to offer.

I felt like the kid with his nose pressed against the window on a hot summer day, unable to go outside and join in the fun the kids in the neighborhood were experiencing: unwilling to pull myself away from the window ending my torture out of fear of missing something monumental. All my friends, family were taking risks in following their dreams, getting married or traveling around the world and I could be found following the same mundane schedule without change. Nia was all that to me but I could not see it at the time; I just wanted more *me-time.*

On the few occasions I managed to get away from Nia, it was similar to the feeling of winning the lottery. My joy would always give way to a sense of guilt stemming from putting my needs before Nia's needs. Asking someone to deal with behaviors that would drive me wild would also factor into my guilt. I did not understand that my feeling of guilt was based on my own inability to break my own routine.

It was early in the morning and Nia was on her way to Summer School. The bus matron had already been hazed by Nia and she greeted my child with a huge smile. Instead of going back upstairs to eat more pancakes prepared by my mother, I stayed in the vestibule of my building shaking my head at what I saw. The front of the entrance of *310* was empty. Only people in the front area of the building were the maintenance men cleaning up the mess left from the night before by the individuals who used the front entrance as a public living room. The cleaning of the front area was a cyclical occurrence. The disregard some showed for the area outside their residence made me think of how they kept their apartments in the same building. As I waited, I watched Nia's longtime babysitter Ms. Marlene leave out of the back of the building with a pushcart apparently going shopping.

Ms. Marlene took excellent care of Nia until she started school. Ms. Marlene would feed Nia meals that I wished someone would cook for me. She was my lifesaver in my darkest moments of getting my bearings on single fatherhood. She would take care of half the children in *310* as well as three of my nephews and my niece. I waived to her and Ms. Marlene waved back as he continued out of the building. I always said if I won the lottery she would be one of the first people I would bless with money.

My stay in the vestibule did not last long because a Black Acura RL careened around the corner of the block at a high rate of speed. The vehicle stopped at the curb directly in front of me. The car was driven by another one of my brothers from another mother and father, Cleveland Roosevelt Woods Junior. Cleve', as he preferred to be called was a year older than me. At a quick glance looked similar to Rapper LL Cool J with the same build. Cleve' also had the habit of rolling up one pant leg like LL did, but if you called him LL Cool J he would get upset and resemble the Hulk. Not many people wanted to upset him.

"Yo' dog, I can't wait for you to see the house" Cleve' yelled from the open window of his car. The car was four years old but the way he took care of his "Black Beauty," it looked brand new. I walked over to the passenger's side and hopped into the seat. We gave each other dap before making my response.

"I'm rolling with a big dog today."

My voice mocked the character Tommy from the Martin Television series. I wanted to see his new house first hand, but just as important I very much needed to take my first trip out of New York City in months. As Cleve' drove to the highway I glanced at my cell phone to mark the time. The countdown to Nia's arriving on the bus began without fanfare.

The hour and one-half ride to upstate New York gave us an opportunity to catch up on lost time. Small talk eventually turned into talk about in the days when we both had nothing but dreams. Our days back then were spent traveling Manhattan Island with just enough money in our pockets to get something to eat and drink. Cleve' and I would head to our many spots including The Village to window shop for clothes and check out the beautiful women we would undoubtedly see on our excursion. We would see fancy cars and the beautiful homes and wish one day we would own the same.

Cleve' and I bet which one of us would be the first to get their apartment, car, child, marriage, and vacation outside the country. At the time, we made the bet it was inconceivable that anyone of us would accomplish more than one item on the list, he with no high school diploma and me with needing to pass sixteen classes in order to graduate in my senior year of high school at John F. Kennedy. Life got in the way of receiving his diploma right away but eventually, he would finish what he started. Riding in his car going upstate to see his new house made me realize that Cleve' had won each of the bets.

"You remember all the bets we made? You won them all" I conceded as I needlessly checked the time on my cell phone just twenty minutes after leaving my block. Cleve' had an immediate response for me.

"You have Nia bro', God will give it to you on his time, not yours."

He preached in his no-nonsense voice. His words of the gospel made him a very interesting individual to know. Everything in his background suggested that he would not be that attuned to the "Good

Word" but he understood the words more than most. In a moment, he could sound like the atypical angry black man: the next moment he could sound like a burgeoning preacher. His complex nature did not stop at words of wisdom it extended to his desire to improve his life.

He managed to land a low-level position with a local electric company and progressed up the ladder until he became an emergency worker splicing high voltage cables. Cleve's job was very dangerous yet very rewarding for him for when he showed up on scene people were usually angry their lights were out. He received offers of apple pie and hugs of gratitude for the work he'd done to restore power. He successfully fought his company for the opportunity to obtain his title making him the first in its history to fight and win. His accomplishments made me want to push hard to progress in life rather than flat line. When Nia's mother was mentioned by me the tone of the conversation changed dramatically.

Cleve' knew a great deal of what went on between Nia's mother and myself: therefore, he had an emotional investment in the matter. Cleve' kept me calm when I should be and he admonished my behavior whenever I was wrong. When he asked me about the welfare of Nia's mother it was not out of concern. "She is doing well. She has a good job and a car" I answered. My voice was devoid of emotion because of the anger I once felt when her name was mentioned in conversation. The years apart took away my anger melting it away with all I had to worry about with Nia. Cleve' felt the need to address the lack of anger on my part.

"Don't need to be that person anymore Cleve'."

"Nobody can blame you Dee."

"I blame myself. I knew better but I chose to do wrong."

"There is no way I can imagine…"

"…You can't so don't try."

I stated. In the court of my conscience I had been given a life sentence. My father always said it takes a man, or for that matter a woman to face up to wrong and in this instance I was a man. The images of my Mr. Hyde impersonations I conducted in the past were strong enough to have me change the subject to a less sorrowful one.

The change of topic did not halt my first real thoughts about Nia's mother in five years.

We arrived in the town of Monroe, New York and quickly made our way to Cleve's property. We had to turn off a two-lane paved road onto a gravel road. Cleve' slowly drove to the top of a hill where his house stood. When we reached the top he parked the car in front of the driveway to his house.

The former owners had the house built to resemble a log cabin. They must have been '*rustics*' because the idea of building and living in a log cabin does not fit the concept of modern housing. Cleve' took me on a long slow tour of his house and property, which included three acres of land as well as a swimming pool next to the house and a babbling stream. Being from the city I had difficulty understanding how large three acres of land was, but the property was large enough to build more houses. As Cleve' showed me around I spent time thinking about what I would do if I were in his place.

In my rendition, there would be room for a bigger pool one that Nia would swim in and I could stand in because I could not swim. I saw the guesthouse I would have to build to accommodate the visitors who would come to the cookouts and parties hosted by me. In the end, my thoughts returned to my running all over the property one dark night looking for Nia. The thought ended my romantic idea of being a homeowner that well north of New York City.

At the end of the tour, we found ourselves in his car preparing to leave when he asked the obvious question.

"What do you think Dee?" He asked with pride.

"I love it!"

I responded still thinking about Nia running out of the door and into the woods.

My sentiment was true; I waited for a hint of jealousy to bubble up in me, but became happy that none appeared. As I opened his car door I once again checked my cell phone that was already in my hand to notice that there were two and one-half hours. Cleve' saw me check the time.

"Do you think you have enough time to get something to eat?" he asked me with concern. I carried a few dollars with me, not enough buy my meal. I hesitated with my answer and Cleve' at once knew the reason for my pause.

"Don't worry about it, I got ya'" Cleve' responded. It reminded me of the times we lent each other money when one of us was very low on funds. We got in his car and headed for a local restaurant for a bit to eat and to continue our discussion. As we drove away from his house I wondered if my sins of the past permanently made all my hopes and dreams on earth liquid to my touch.

The food was good, and the conversation was even better. We spoke about the good old days again this time with an eye on the future. Somewhere during the conversation, my internal clock went off and I checked my cell phone. We talked away all the time I allotted as a buffer for getting Nia off the bus on time. Cleve' saw the look on my face and knew that time was more imperative than I let on. He called for the check and we left the dinner bound for Manhattan and reestablishing of my daily routine. My mother was at church and only I could get Nia.

The ride back to Manhattan was filled with even more conversation than on the way up. Killer called me on my phone and the three of us joked on one another for a good while before Killer had to exit the conversation to prepare for choir rehearsal. Once again, I silently thanked God for the friends he gave me.

We arrived at my block five minutes before Nia's scheduled dropped off time. I was so overcome by relief that I was not going to be late picking her up. One of my greatest worries was that I would be late enough that Nia would have to be taken to the nearest police precinct where I would have to pick her up and face the Police. When Cleve' turned the corner, I was surprised to see the school bus was in the process of pulling away with Nia still onboard. Cleve' beeped his horn and flashed his lights which caught the bus driver's attention and he stopped. The driver was five minutes early and I could not understand why he was prepared to leave.

I gave Cleve' dap then leaped out of his car to run over to the bus. The doors to the bus opened and the matron exited the bus with a look of profound disgust on her face.

"I don't know what happened to her today?'

The woman said, with frustration oozing from her voice. She did not give me a chance to give my usual greeting before she spoke, which gave further sign Nia was out of order in school or on the bus or both. Nia followed the matron off the bus. Her eyes were as big as ever another sign her behavior was not the best. The fun I had on the trip quickly was erased. Anger took its place for Nia could not go back to her mischievous days.

Each time Nia's bus was changed there was a period of adjustment that needed to happen to her. She was taken off the large bus because she would take off her seatbelt each time the bus would stop and run the length of the bus. Once she taught the kids on the long bus how to remove their seat belts and run the length of the bus with her. She was a leader but not in the way I would prefer. Each matron would insist that I get a bus paraprofessional for her at the start of the run and by the end, they all expressed a genuine like for my budding anarchist.

As Nia came off the bus and I took hold of her hand and held a strong grip I wished she could explain to me the circumstances that caused the matron anguish, but some wishes would never come true. I addressed the matron before we parted ways.

"I will call the school to find out what was wrong."

I assured the matron. I made sure to let the driver know that he was early and they did have my cell phone number, then lead Nia toward the building. I looked back to see the bus blocked Cleve' from moving and I gave him the peace sign. Nia and I walked to the steps of the building and made our way up, all the while Nia continued to have a worried look on her face. The instant I opened the door to enter the building I realized why Nia kept a look of worry. Her shirt was on backward and turned inside out. Nia's socks were turned inside out as well and her shoelaces were untied. It was clear that at some point in her day, Nia might have been shirtless and barefoot in school. The thought of which was intolerable.

"Why is your shirt on inside out and backward Nia?"

I growled in a low but angry tone. She still took off her clothes when she became angry. There would not be a response coming from Nia but I need to ask. Nia, let out a cry, which equaled a normal child telling their parents to "Leave them alone." She knew better than tell me to leave her alone.

"I told you not to take off your clothes at school ever again" I scolded Nia as we rounded the corner to the elevator. She once again in her way told me to leave her alone. There was no one in the lobby and at the time, which did not matter to me. I was not going to let the episode pass without correction. I took another look to make sure the coast was clear before a frantically put her shirt on the proper way ahead of anyone entering the lobby. I was thankful to have the good sense to send her to school in the summer with a tank top on under her shirt for just this type of situation however there was no way to know if that came off as well.

I pressed for the elevator and the thought of my child running around her school half-dressed popped into my head. The next thought in my mind was why no one in the school had alerted me to the behavior. I could not get my answers from anyone in the school nor from Nia. We entered the elevator and my anger had not subsided.

"I told you not to take off your clothes. You know better Nia!"

My voice was filled with anger when I spoke this time. Nia reacted to my anger by biting her forearm hard enough to leave teeth marks. She had not done this to herself in years and like the last time she bit herself I popped her in her mouth. Convinced that I had extinguished the unwanted behavior for the moment I let her arm free. The elevator ride was unusually fast this day but the instant the elevator door opened Nia ran off screaming toward our apartment door. I tried to grab her, but she was able to break away.

Just before she reached our door she managed to do a baseball slide ending at our door. I ran after her and reached her just as her Jeter like slide ended and snatched her up off the floor. I very much wanted to ring her neck by this time, but I was able to control myself. When she was young these episodes would occur with much more frequency and the duration could last hours.

My response may not meet the approval of many, but my actions did bring [to] an end to the regularity of such occurrences.

I could not allow the clock to be rewound because Nia was older and could do much more damage to her person. I would do everything

103

in my powers to prevent her from harming herself and others. As I pulled her into the apartment Nia began to rub her leg from the floor burn she gave herself from the Jeter slide. The tough work of coping with Nia, made me promise God to find a solution to her outburst as soon as humanly possible. Dealing with her made me see things in people that others did not see.

DOUBLE EDGE SWORD

In the realm of parenting, there is no substitute for experience. The idea of having gone through something once before gives one the thread of possibility of what may happen. All new parents, as well as seasoned veterans, learn as they go, gaining needed experience based on the experience they accumulate. Mistakes are bound to occur; don't be afraid to make them. Like my former Pastor used to say, there is no such thing as mistakes only bad choices.

There is nothing more entertaining for me than to listen to experts claim to have the key to raising a "well-behaved child." First and foremost, we all know there is no definitive book or website that holds all the answers parents seek. If there were there would be an entire group of children raised to believe the same thing and react to situations in the same manner. This would not be raising children but rather raising like-minded drones, not individuals. Raising a child is a type of limited partnership between parent and child. The limited part comes from how much input the parent allows the child to have in the relationship.

Generally speaking, the child is supposed to do as the parent says because the parent owns the life experience that the child does not fully understand *action's* consequence. An infant is on its own schedule regulated by the need to sleep, be changed and to eat. Parents are at the mercy of the infant. As the child turns into a toddler some parents start the process of molding their child to fit their own schedule. Where the conflict lies is when the expectations of the parents collide with the interest of the child.

My Uncle Charles used a phrase to keep his grandchildren Shanek, Shawn and Shannon in-line when they displayed behavior that was not to his liking. The phrase was "Mind Your Character." Those three words were a powerful reminder to my cousins to practice the behaviors he expected in the absence of authority. It was a sort of 'grandfather is watching you' that worked well for him. My cousins knew what was expected of them and the relationship in that area was solid. Sometimes warnings were not sufficient to establish the boundaries to the parent-child relationship.

My sister Kim took another approach to establishing the parent-child relationship with her three children. Circumstances of being a single mother made my sister demand that her children not challenge her authority. She *dared* her children Lettisha, Dawan, and Taliah to get out of line: which they were wise enough not to call her to action. Her technique worked well for her. Their outcomes were the result of her teaching practices.

My Uncle Charlie and my sister Kim did not act out of vengeance, caring was the main motivator. In the end, they explained in these cases where the ends justifies the means, as long as you, the parent did not act out of anger or vengeance toward the child: the child could accept what you did. If you act because you care the child will one day understand why the action taken was necessary, because at the proper time you would explain yourself to the child. The reason why a good parent would explain to their child is that they would gain experience to pass on.

Children quickly adapt to the ways their parents discipline them. The child that is hit for every infraction forms his/her character shaped on emotions, which arise during the beatings. The child who is only spoken to learns how to tune out prolonged one-sided discussions. The child who is given freedom to challenge the partnership may grow to devalue authority as an adult. There is no science to what I say however I watched how many of my friends were raised and I understand what could happen and from my point of view too much of anything is bad. My father used to recite "everything in moderation." Whenever I reveled in the good I would do. When it comes to Nia I used every method available in moderation, whatever it took to get her to act within limits. My goal was not to vent my anger but to avoid her doing something on the street that might put her in danger.

I learned from experience that a good parent must set standards and be an excellent juggler. The older the child becomes the more input into the relationship should be bestowed upon the child until that child is an adult on its own. Your child may have more or less cognitive abilities than Nia, but they all have feelings and display emotions: be mindful of what you say because kids 'lock-into' the good and bad with a vice grip. No matter if you believe my words, I do say as a parent to mind your character and if that doesn't work draw that line in the sand - but remember everything in moderation.

Before You Let Go

Being able to let go is the most challenging lesson any good parent must face. Each stage of a child's life there will come a time when the idea of letting the child go will scare the heck out of the parent. Whether it is taking off the training wheels on the bike or letting your child choose their college, parents struggle with trusting when is the time to let go of their child. As for my situation, I had trouble knowing if I should let go of her.

Once I was accustomed to the everyday routine of caring for Nia it became a matter of reflex. There was no thought involved to what needed to be done for Nia; all that was needed was the energy to get that particular job done. I did not recognize the amount of damage I was doing to myself because I did not want to count on anyone rejecting my request for help. Nia's communication skills did not improve with age and the idea of someone taking advantage of her was ever present.

I waited for the day when she could talk which would release my fears about spending more time without her. My dreams did not come true and Nia's preteen behaviors, crying hysterically when I left her with someone, temper tantrums when she wanted to leave whatever place we were could be attributed to having just me in her life. She knew how I would react both positively and negatively, and Nia would do things to get my attention. There was no way of telling if Nia understood right from wrong, or the consequences of actions which made it difficult at times to know what to do when she did things I knew were not safe or right for her to do.

I grew up in the neighborhood in which we lived and knew a great many people. Whenever I had Nia in tow and would stop to run my mouth with someone, she would squat down like a catcher in baseball. If that did not get my attention Nia would then lay out on the sidewalk which definitely would get my undivided attention. Nia was used to being the center of attention for me and when anyone took my attention off her too long she wanted it back.

From the time her mother left, I did not want to be the only parent in her life. I wanted her to need more than just me, but when that did not work out I decided to find programs in the city that would bring her around other adults and have her be near other kids with developmental disorders.

Caring for people with special needs in the 21st Century was much different from how the "Mentally Retarded" of the late Mid-19th Century were treated. Gone was the warehousing in institutions like Willowbrook on Staten Island which Geraldo Rivera exposed in the early 1970s. Children with Special Needs were kept out of the public eye out of shame or other reasons. During Nia's lifetime the amount of programs and strategies increased and gave me and other like parents opportunities to improve our lives and the lives of our children.

Depending on the city in which one lives, there should be organizations that help parents of Special Needs children with the things that would make life easier. I found during my search some organizations deal with specific needs while others cover the gambit. In New York City, the number of agencies and the services offered by the agencies allow for organizations to exists that can help parents find the services they want and need.

The need for a Service Coordinator gave me the ability to suggest the services I wanted and the Service Coordinator would search to find the agency that could provide my needs. I was able to sign up for a reimbursement program that gives one back up to five hundred dollars of clothes I purchased for Nia. One can get discounts on apartments based on salary and number of people living with the Special Needs Child. I was able to find peer groups that served as places for parents to share and vent if needed. It is possible to find the information on one's own but I found it better to have someone look for me because my free time was very limited.

The service coordinator informed me of a program called *Respite*. As the title shows, the parent would get a respite from the child and the child from the overbearing parent. The idea of trusting Nia with strangers put me off for a few seconds before I loudly exclaimed, "Sign me up!" The people who would deal with Nia were professionals who would have experience dealing with all types of behaviors including the ones showed by Nia. I walked away from that meeting shaking my head at the thought of Nia being kicked out of the program because she was being herself. I had to try something.

To understand you do not have to be alone in the daily struggles of taking care of a Special Needs Child is to open yourself to chance and opportunity. The experience learned from both parent and child. Some of us parents of these children never learn to trust in anyone but themselves, therefore, their child may not experience all life has to offer. Once being one of those people, I never thought of anyone doing for my child what I could, however, there could never be another me they could only be who they were. In the end, I had to put my trust in strangers and in Nia and hope for the best. Once the change was a foreign entity in my life, but now I had embarked on a journey of change.

CHAPTER 13

While change was not a major part of my experience with Nia the same could not be said for my life as a New York City School Teacher. The day came when I was excessed from Chelsea High School. While at Chelsea I lost my niece Marie. She did not have the opportunity to let out her first cry before God called her home. My father, who held out hope to see his grandchild born, instead Marie went up to heaven ahead of him. He was diagnosed with lung cancer and brushed aside the insistence of the doctor to give up smoking while he was being treated.

"I can only die once" he defiantly told the doctor as he continued to smoke until he was unable. Lastly, Nia's mother finally exited our lives while I worked at the school. Leaving Chelsea meant leaving experiences both positive and negative. I made a brief stop at Jacqueline Kennedy Onassis High School found in the heart of the Theater and Diamond Districts. At the school the movie "Fame" was based on, I learned new techniques that improved my delivery of information as well as my assessment of the students. The antics of the infamous principal at J.K.O. made being excessed from the school more of a relief than the annoyance of having to remain in the building tending to the closed library until I was assigned to another school.

In those days when a teacher was excessed from a school the central board would identify a school in need of a teacher in your license area. You would be placed in by seniority: the person with the least would be "bumped out" of their position. Don't feel too bad for the teacher that got bumped. It was easy to find a job in those days, no one went without work unless they were not likable or did not know how to run an effective classroom.

During my transit to the new school, I called Killer on the phone to inform him where I would be teaching. I was surprised that he was working at Bayard Rustin High School for The Humanities, through the organization Coalition Council. It was a program that taught the principles of nonviolence teaching self-esteem to mostly at risk students. Bryant was perfect for that position.

"Yo' Dee. You will fit in here"

Killer enthusiastically guaranteed. The idea of working with Killer, my good friend was very intriguing. During my long walk to my new job location I began to process some very interesting facts that had me talking to myself. Irony played a prominent role in my life as a teacher, because the names of each of the schools I worked in had a real life connection.

Dr. Martin Luther King Jr. was advised by Bayard Rustin. It was Bayard Rustin who wrote much of the "I Have a Dream Speech" Dr. King eloquently delivered during the March On Washington. Both men met with Jacqueline Kennedy, wife of President John F. Kennedy, to discuss the Civil Rights issues. Bayard Rustin, was a gay Black man who enjoyed the company of younger white men. The school is located in Chelsea, a predominately gay white neighborhood on Manhattan Island. Armed with all that irony I began my march to a fresh start at the former Charles Evans Hughes High School, the first high school I attended way, way back in 1980.

When I walked through the doors of Bayard Rustin memories of my first day attending Charles Evans Hughes High School, its former name came to my recollection. My mother escorted me to the school on the first day of Ninth Grade and we were greeted with the sight and smell of weed being smoked on school property. Neither of us was prepared for what else would come during my stay at the historically bad school. It was the same school my older cousin Charles attended years earlier. It was a tough school when he attended and there was very little change on my first day.

Six months after my mother escorted me to the school she returned with transfer papers for the Principal Mr. Whitestone to sign. My mother was ready for a fight because she had to do just that to get the transfer from the Board of Education to the school I wanted to attend. My mother and I managed to corner the unsuspecting principal on the first floor of the building. The look on my mother's face showed the principal she meant she would accept nothing less than what she wanted. The principal asked why she was there and her response was to "transfer my son." His response was not what either of us was prepared to hear. He took the papers from my mother and used her back to sign them on the spot.

"I don't blame your mother" he said upon handing the papers back to my mother. Off to John F Kennedy High School, I went, never to think about Charles Evans Hughes until I walked through the door two decades later. The lobby looked the same as it did those many years earlier. There was a security desk to the left of the lobby and as I approached the officer to identify myself I heard a loud commotion coming from the other side of a large metal door. Seconds later the door was thrown open with great force which startled me and a group of students preparing to go on a trip.

A student was forcibly escorted to the Dean's office by staff members. His foul mouth preceded his coming through the door which did not end once he was on my side of the door. He resisted every inch of the way. In that instant, I took a deep breath and proclaimed I was home.

I learned from my unofficial mentor at MLK High School the main person to know in any school was the Payroll Secretary and the second person to know was the custodian.

"The Payroll Secretary handles your money; the custodian can open any door for you" my mentor informed me. I followed his instructions and had a long talk with the Payroll Secretary before meeting Killer in his office. Meeting the custodian would take place another day. Killer was happy to see me and immediately introduced me to two teachers, Barbara Williams and Sandhi Ortiz. We formed an immediate bond which would only be broken by death.

At the end of the first day, I stood in front of the huge half block long seven-story building hoping this would be the place I could teach until I retired. Stability at work could only benefit me at home.

I could now pay closer attention to Nia without dealing with all the changes that came with moving to a new school. I knew if I could not put Nia on the bus in the morning my mother could, the same scenario would play out in the afternoon. There was now time for me to put in place the plan for Nia I had long put off.

CHAPTER 14

Bayard Rustin High School was just the place I had longed for in my teaching career. It was a very large building with a large student body. In its heyday, there were nearly three thousand students and over one hundred and fifty adults in the building. The large student body allowed me the opportunity to teach a variety of history classes that weren't Special Education.

The location of the school made getting to and from work easy for me. I did not have to bother my mother to get Nia off the bus because I enrolled Nia in the after-school program that kept her until six PM Monday through Friday. The After-school Program allowed Nia the opportunity to burn off energy. It also gave me more time to prepare for her arrival as well as get some school work done. It was not long before the city, cut funding to allow only four days a week. Parents like myself were sent scrambling to find support for one day a week. Fridays became an extended weekend day. I had to get Nia out of the house and on the train or to the park.

The closed door that brought change to my life also kept me on a predictable path at work. In six short months, I was made Dean after I witnessed two students stomp out another student in the stairwell. All I can remember is the victim screaming out for help and my peering through the window into the stairwell as the aggressors ran off. The experience of Dean was slightly different from my prior school.

For one thing, the Humanities building was twice the size of Chelsea with twice as many students. There were seven floors to patrol as well as a basement pool area. I prevented many students from doing interesting things in the basement. The position of Dean allowed me the opportunity to roam a huge building that I came to love. In the decade plus stay there the elevator was used sparingly by me. I walked many miles in that time. The occasions that found me using the elevator where to escort students to and from the Dean's Office. Moving about between classes proved once again to be therapeutic for me. The more people I ran into during my travels the less I would think about my troubles at home. I did not realize it at the time, but solving the smallest problem for someone else was my way of dealing with Nia. Helping others was what made me make sense out of my sometimes-hectic days.

The student body of the school was as diverse as the city it called home. It was a trend that would end when certain parties decided that large comprehensive high schools were relics of the past. The stories I heard about the school prior to my arrival made me jealous of what I was not about to experience. Again, I missed out on a good thing but what I witnessed was nothing to 'scoff-at' either. The diversity had me learning how to say words in several languages. At one point, I learned how to say "Close your mouth" in five languages and "Good morning" in six, which was the extent of my linguistic prowess. I wished I'd learned how to say "stop fighting" in another language.

The change of periods was always the most chaotic time of the school day. Thousands of individuals poured out of their classrooms and spilled into the hallways in route to their next class within the five minutes allotted. The main stairwell was not the one to use if anyone wanted to be on time. Ten times each day Grand Central Station during rush hour happened in the main stairwell. Getting into and out of it was always a matter of timing, either by being late or early.

I exited my third-period classroom to wade into a sea of loud teenagers hoping not to get stopped and asked questions. To increase my chances of slinking away I made my way to Stairwell D in the back of the building and in no time, I walked through the door of the Dean's Office not to a question but a statement by the Secretary who worked in the Dean's Office.

"I was just about to call you over the radio" she said as she gave me that all too familiar look that I may have forgotten my radio again. I believed it was in my knapsack and checked inside to make sure that I was right. She went ahead to explain why I arrived just in time.

"You have the parent of James waiting to see you" she announced as she pointed to the woman seated in the waiting area in the office. There was no need for the last name because I called her countless times on the phone about the behavior of her son. Her visit was a surprise because he was never in any big trouble at school but he did hang around troubled kids.

"I finally get a chance to meet the person behind the voice" I said as I walked over to her and extended my hand showing her the way into my private office. She followed my direction and she took a seat in my cubby hole of an office. Wood made up three sides of the office and the back wall was made of concrete. The space was converted into offices out of one large office space. Seven individuals shared the space with me which made the term "My Office" laughable. I placed my knapsack on an unoccupied chair and my attention belonged to the mother. What she confided in me had me thinking of Nia.

She came to the school that day convinced that she was going to send her son to his father's home country to live with his father. She felt her son was out of control and he needed discipline she was unable to give him. She looked no more than thirty-five years old if that which meant she was not much older than her son. She was dressed in the uniform of an airport ticket agent which I assumed meant long hours away from her son. I sat quietly listening, her voice filled with frustration. Her frustrations were not eased when reminded that the calls home were about his lateness to school and to class and not for doing something violent or disrespectful to an adult.

"I don't understand him. We live in a house and he has every game system out. I did this to keep him from stealing and then he gets caught stealing in the local bodega multiple times."

She confessed. There were no tears on her part; she wanted to be sure of how he was doing in school before she shipped him out to live with his father. I looked at the woman and did not pull [in] party-line talk on her. I spoke as if I were a man of color and not just an educator concerned with averages and college aspiration for her son.

"You have to do what is best for your son. You know him better than anyone."

I reasoned as I left the room to get the mother her son's attendance information. Upon my return I asked the polite question of the state in the south her son would live with his father. The mother gave me that look mothers give when the devil spoke.

"Has he been telling everyone he is from the South again?"

She asked.

"He claimed to have just moved from the south only a few years ago."

I mentioned as I replayed the conversation her son and I had on life in the south.

"He fooled me. I had to speak to him about making fun of a girl because she wore African attire."

The mother understood the reason for the confusion.

"My family names are Wilson, but we are from West Africa. His father is from the Caribbean. He had every adult in his Junior High School fooled as well."

She explained. I quickly turned the conversation to academics which I was sure there would be little surprises. Her son's transcript showed that he was behind in credits, his grades were mostly failing and his cut record showed he missed his first and last period classes. Overall, he was not doing well. While we talked I called him to the office and the moment he walked through my office door he was shocked to see his mother. Immediately he began to speak their native tongue. The irony in his speaking to his mother in an African language was that I admonished him for making fun of a young girl for speaking to him in the same language. I don't remember seeing him again after the meeting, but I know the mother did what was best for herself and her child.

I went home that night thinking of how this mother gave her soul to her child only to have him not appreciate what she gave up for him. Nia could never be a disappointment to me in the way the young man surely disappointed his mother.

CHAPTER 15

The meeting with the parent took place in the early spring and there were no more sports for me to coach. The Boys Junior Varsity Basketball ended with a winning record which was the first that team had in many years. The Boys Varsity Basketball Season ended with an ugly loss in the semifinal game for the City Championship. We lost, rather had the game taken from us on a last second made three point-shot by our player that was waved off by one of three referees.

In my opinion, the referee made a poor call ran off the court without consulting either of his colleagues nor the league officials who knew the call was wrong. Everyone associated with the team, especially Sandhi, took the loss very hard. A win would have added to her basketball 'legend' as the first female coaching boys in New York City to win the Championship. The loss bothered me as well because a win would have made me a champion at something other than dreaming big. There was nothing left to distract me from what *'going home'* meant in the fullest sense.

I left my office sure that I did not leave anything of importance behind. I hurriedly went about my task of walking the halls of the building, clearing it of loitering students. Instead of waiting for all of them to leave, I quickly checked and hurried to my office to gather my things. I pushed aside the conversation with the mother and her son, and put the loss of the game away for another day. I had an extra sense of energy about me that no ill-tempered student or crotchety staff member could have dampened. I was about to set off on a new adventure that I was not sure how it would end.

I stepped into the lobby of the building to find Killer Bee, and Barbara standing around the security desk. They were chatting away until Killer Bee saw me.

"Are you nervous about today?" Killer asked with his serious voice. I confided in him what I planned to do and he was not sure if I would be alright going through with it. Ms. Williams who stood next to him chimed in with a joke. She was a veteran teacher with a heart of gold who I often went to for advice in teaching Social Studies and life in general. Ms. Williams had a wonderful sense of humor but more importantly she was a spiritual person who one day would become a pastor. Her pastoral duties would help her through two very difficult chapters in her life.

"Don't go making any more babies Darryl" she announced, as she and Killer laughed loudly.

"There ain't a chance of that happening. I was spayed last week" I answered back. Then realized the mistake I made but it was too late the laughter had already started. I sometimes thought too fast and misspoke: this was one of those times. We talked for a minute as Killer and Barbara were waiting for another person to join them for an after-work bite to eat. The third member was Sandhi Ortiz. Some people are said to be "One in a million" Sandhi was not included in that mix. There was no way to quantify her as a person. You had to see and hear to believe her.

Sandhi was and is a basketball *'legend'* in and out New York City. Her skills in basketball saw her inducted in the Hall of Fame at the Rucker Park in Harlem as well as City College Of New York. Her skills made her an excellent referee, good enough in fact the National Basketball Association considered making her the first female referee in the Association before the glass ceiling was placed over her head. At one point she was the only female to coach a Boys Varsity Basketball Team in New York City; with all that fame she was as equally famous for what might come out of her mouth.

She would say things that would peel paint off the walls but it was all in fun. At first glance Sandhi was a tiger, but if you were allowed to get close she was a Teddy Bear.

"Who are you going to be whoring with tonight?" Sandhi said without shame.

"Remember to stretch out before you try any wild positions." "You know you have a bad back" she added. The students never heard her speak that way and if they did they would not believe she spoke that way. I had to join in the laughter but I needed to set the record straight.

"Those days are long gone" I remorsefully answered. There was more I wanted to say on the topic but there was not enough time. I excused myself and headed for home before I was dragged into a long but interesting conversation. The further away I got from Bayard Rustin and the drama the school day brought, the giddier I became about the new adventure that awaited me. I sat on the A train tired but too nervous to go to sleep.

I arrived home in enough time to get a suitcase from the apartment and still make Nia's bus on time. The moment Nia exited the bus I inspected her clothes and was pleased to find they were on the right way however her shoelaces were untied. After the last wardrobe incident I contacted her school and impressed upon them the need to tell me when Nia acted inappropriately. I had to pick my battles, therefore I just made mention of Nia taking off her shoes to the matron and taking off her clothes before we started on our way to our weekend destination. Nia wanted to run up the ramp to the building, which was her custom but I stopped her in mid-stride.

"I told you we had somewhere to go Nia" I informed her as I knelt down to tie her shoes. She knew something was going on because I had her suitcase with me.

"I told you we're going to **Respite** today."

Nia's blank look made me wonder if she understood my words. The process to get Nia into Weekend Respite was long enough in the making that I forgot about the application. I was apprehensive about sending Nia to strangers but it was my mother who convinced me to trust in God and let go. This would be my first day away from Nia in eight years, yet I wondered why I did not feel any anxiety about dropping my child off with strangers. We made our way up Bradhurst Avenue. I had a little trouble with the rolling suitcase staying upright. I stopped on the corner of 145th to check to see if there was anything that could be done to keep it on its wheels when Ms. Daisy Lee, a neighbor in my building came upon us. She had a shocked look on her face as she realized I pulled a suitcase behind me.

"Where are you going Darryl?" she asked me.

"I'm not going anywhere but Nia is going away for the weekend" I said as I wrangled the suitcase on its wheels.

"Good for you Darryl" Ms. Daisy Lee said in a happy voice. When she caught her breath she added, "what do you plan to do with your time off?"

"Nothing special" I responded. Ms. Daisy Lee looked at me and said, "That is all right, you need your rest."

"God Bless you baby" she said as she renewed her trek to the building. For once, Nia did not try to curtail my conversation by her usual means of lying down on the sidewalk or trying to pull away from me. Her lack of action surprised me but it was a pleasure to able to talk without dividing my attention. Having no special plans almost made me cancel her appointment at The Young Adult Institute YAI, but canceling would be a selfish act on my part. We stopped on the corner of 145th and Edgecombe Avenue and looked down the block to 144th Street out of habit. I tried to teach Nia how to cross the street but I was not confident she could achieve the task on her own.

We crossed the street and made our way to the subway station. Many of my life's milestone event began upon entering that very station. The suitcase tilting over several times interrupted the walk. We turned on St. Nicholas Avenue; and were confronted by a line weaving its way down the block with people waiting to buy fish. The long lines continued to be the norm. Down the stairs we went and Nia began to giggle as she did whenever we went downtown on the train. As we boarded the Local C train Nia immediately pulled me to the seat closest to the window. Taking my seat next to her, I placed the suitcase between my legs to keep if from moving during stops and starts. The door closed and the train started to move as did the suitcase start to role.

Nia acted normally during our train ride downtown. She looked out the window of the train at the passing stations and held her ever-present piece of paper in her hand. I searched for signs of distress on her part but there were none. She displayed her happy normal laughter and pretty wide face smile. There was no way to tell if she would have one of her classic meltdowns at Respite the moment I left, if she did it would trouble me greatly.

Taking the local train instead of the express train made for a longer ride because I did not want to arrive too early for our appointed time. I had a thing for arriving places early with Nia because she still had a problem with waiting. The longer ride time gave me the opportunity to reflect on how much Nia had grown enough to allow me to feel that she was ready to spend a night with strangers, not family.

My eldest Nephew Mario Jr. once made the same observation of Nia a few years earlier. At that time Nia had dropped many of her habits as well as her propensity to cry each time I left the room. It was as if her behaviors had become more tolerable but more likely we had gotten used to who she was and how her disability affected her. Mario said one day Nia would change enough that would allow her to be around people other than family. Seeing Nia on the train gave me *goosebumps*, because I could have never imagined this day ever happening.

We exited the train at a familiar stop 14th Street and Eighth Avenue. Nia had gone with me to work on many occasions, therefore she was not the least bit surprised to exit at that station. Instead of heading in the direction of work on 18th Street we walked west along 16th Street passing the park where many of the kids that attended my school cut class.

The park was a haven for students to play handball, basketball or have a fight when they should be in school learning. Each time I walked by the park I scanned for students which became a bothersome behavior for me. In all the time I worked at Humanities, I didn't pay any attention to the nondescript red brick building walkup that was adjacent to park. I rang the bell and waited to be buzzed into the building. I glanced back at the park once again and remembered the face of the boy who returned to school bloodied by a fight, and turned my attention back to Nia who giggled as she mumbled to herself.

We were buzzed into the building and we made our way up the narrow flights of stairs the suitcase banging against each step on the way up. I got tired of the banging and carried it up the rest of the way. The interior of the building was as plain as its exterior. Dark colored carpet accented with dark colored paint on the walls made the place less cheerful than it could be. Nia and I arrived on the third floor to find a door ajar. Peering in the small glass window on the door I saw two young girls about Nia's age, sitting on a red couch. I pushed open the door and entered the apartment hoping that I made the right choice.

The two workers one male one female who approached us as soon as we entered immediately greeted us. The first impression rested much of my fears. They walked me over to a nearby table where we began the intake process while Nia made her way over to the couch where the two young girls sat. She looked very comfortable as if she were making fast friends at a local coffee house.

The intake process took about twenty minutes. I signed my name several dozen times and with each signature I looked over at Nia in anticipation of the moment that was about to come. At my completion of the intake forms I casually made my way toward the door wondering when Nia would start her performance at first sign of my departure. The plan was to walk out without saying anything to her but that was the punk way out. I stopped just short of the door and turned towards Nia who was still seated on the couch. Uncertain of what response I would receive I raised my hand in Nia's direction and uttered the words I hoped would not send her into frenzy.

"Bye Nia" I said. She looked up at me and responded in staccato.

"Bye" Nia said as she waved her hand. All my worries were wiped away in an instant. I left the apartment stunned at how she reacted and trying to see where I went wrong with worry. I stood out in front of the building for a moment and took a deep breath of foul New York City air and wondered what I would do with my newfound freedom. All my peeps were busy for the night and since I had no semblance of a love life, I was left to wander the city until I was ready to head home duty free for at least two nights. At least for the next day and a half I would have time to grade papers and get ready for work on Monday. Nia had left my side for the first time in ten years; I was happy but lost at the same time.

CHAPTER 16

My time off from Nia went by quickly enough that I wanted to send her to **Respite** a second time sooner rather than later. Her absence gave me the opportunity to feel as I did when I was childless: when seeking pleasure and not money was my driving force. My goals had gathered dust as did my swag. I did not have much of either to begin with, but it was enough that I could entice a female into giving me her phone number. The time I spent taking care of Nia drained all desire of companionship from my essence. She would have to take Nia and I as a lifetime package deal, and I assumed not many women were up to the task. I was guilty of doing the thing many overwhelmed parents do, relegating their needs to another day.

There came a time when I had but one coat for winter and two pairs of shoes for the same season. Several eagled-eyed students called me out on the fact I wore the same boots day after day. I had no answer I wanted to give them. This was a far cry from when I could go one month without wearing the same anything twice: shoes, pants or shirt. When I did manage to pick up an item for myself I found any reason to feel guilty and put it down and replaced it with something for Nia who expected to go shopping each weekend. My shopping for Nia paid unexpected dividends.

Nia's vocabulary soon included the major stores that lined 34th Street Herald Square as well as the name of the "World's Largest Department Store." While I was encouraged at her expanding use of words, my financial situation made it difficult for me to buy everything I believed she needed. The more we shopped the more contact she had with the sales staff of various stores. Nia and I would be greeted with broad smiles and it gave me a sense of pride that we were recognized from the many patrons that entered the store. During one trip to a shoe store I was made to realize that "I" had to factor into the "We" that was Nia and me.

"May I have this in a size four?' I asked the saleswoman as I held the shoe I wanted for Nia over my head. Nia sat quietly on the seat in front of me. I learned never to take my eye off of her in crowded stores because I was afraid that she could run from me and get lost in the crowd. The sales woman walked over to me and looked at the bottom of the shoe for the lot number. She memorized the number then placed the shoe back where I got it from. She turned around then asked me if I wanted something for myself?

"No, I am just shopping for my daughter."

Of course, I lied. I wanted a brand-new pair of sneakers I ogled for the past month but once more I convinced myself that taking care of my needs would somehow be the improper thing for me to do.

"You always buy your daughter something, but you get nothing for you" the young lady stated. It sounded to me as if she had enough of my cavalier attitude. I made a silent calculation of my finances and I concluded that I did not have enough money to buy for us both, therefore Nia would once again get and I would go without. My hesitation brought about a rebuttal of my thoughts from the sales woman.

"I will give you my discount" she asserted.

"You have to do for her but you must also look out for yourself too."

She said as she walked over to the sneakers I wanted remembering the time I went to pay for them then changed my mind at the last instant.

"Size eleven, right?"

She gave me a look that forced me to nod my head in the affirmative. Once I put the sneakers on my feet I recalled how it was to grant my own wishes. That experience started me thinking about other aspects of my life I neglected to fulfill, and how I would rekindle my swag.

The purchase of the sneakers did not hasten my transformation from out of date to up to date. The change came slowly but it needed to happen in order for me to remember that I should not lose myself in duties as father to Nia. The shopping trips continued and I was amazed at the new words spoken by Nia. Sometimes I would ask her where she wanted to go just in case she would respond. Her eyes would sometimes dart back and forth as she worked matters out in her mind.

My question sometimes had to be repeated more than once before she would give her one word response to me. There were times she would say the train line she wanted to ride to which I would ask her the stop we would get off the train. My reason for this was that I hoped she would be able to tell me what she wanted which would show a great deal of understanding on her part. It would take years for Nia to respond with a definitive answer, but until then I continued to treat her as if I would a "normal" child as I began to treat myself as her equal. There would always be times I had to sacrifice but I learned not to sacrifice my needs.

CHAPTER 17

When the good Lord decides to call me home on my tombstone in place of my name will be inscribed the words *Dependable* and *Forgetful* and *Uncle*.' Since I had very little money and virtually no time to do anything I often found myself at home. I was as stationary as a rock on the bottom of a deep lake, until moved by some sort of seismic event. The seismic event was often a telephone call.

After work and even on weekends I could be found at home if I was not walking around the city taking pictures like a common tourist until Nia arrived home from her Saturday program at United Cerebral Palsy, making her only day off Sunday. Our trips around the city on weekends still took place but after she arrived home on Saturday. If one is an accessible adult then there will always be someone finding something for you to do.

I did not mind very much that I was the unofficial go-to guy for Jackie and my niece Vonnetta to watch their kids. I enjoyed seeing kids grow and behave in a way I would ever experience from Nia. I could suffer through the intolerable back and forth conversations as well as the infernal question of "Why" being asked of me by the sweet kiddies. There was a sense of wonderment on my part whenever they did something most parents would call annoying. Being with them my niece and my nephews and Nia at the same time opened their eyes to her condition.

My wildest dream would have been able to watch all my nieces and nephews play with Nia as I rocked back and forth on the porch of my mini-mansion I bought after hitting the lottery. Since dreams were not living entities, I settled for watching them gallivant in the local playground as I sat watching from a park bench. I had to teach and not preach about Nia's disability. My first chance came via an open question.

"How come Nia doesn't talk?" my Great Niece Jazmine Simone, asked me about Nia not responding to her question. Jasmine's voice was filled with concern as if Nia did not like her. I remember explaining to Jazmine about Nia suffering from Autism, not exactly in those words, but in language a child of seven years of age could understand. Jazmine listened to my explanation at its end she looked at me with her big brown eyes than simply said something to Nia that floored me.

"That's O.K that you can't talk to me. I still love you, Nia" Jazmine announced then gave Nia a hug. Nia responded at that time with a rare smile. Sometimes great wisdom comes from the innocent. From that day on she never gave Nia's disability a second thought. Jasmine's reaction was heartwarming but she was not the only young person in my family who would come into contact with Nia. It took as much time for Nia to adjust to them, as they would have to adjust to her.

Years after the incident with Jazmine, my sister Jackie gave birth to her twin sons. Their birth also marked the upcoming "next time" I would have to explain Nia's disability to another relative. When Jackie's twins were four years old they began to ask questions about Nia and her behaviors. Unlike Jazmine, the questions did not stop with one explanation. It took many years and many talks for them not to ask about why Nia acted in a manner they were not accustomed to. My twin nephews were not being rude by asking the same question over and over again. The twins showed me that everyone would deal with Nia differently especially young children. They were too young to know but from the time they were infants whenever they cried it would have an effect upon Nia. She would jump on the couch then slam her back against the back. I helped pay for two couches in the time a lived with my mother. When it came to adults, the adjustment period seemed much longer.

Say what you want; not everyone adjusts quickly to new situations. Some dive straight in while others wade into the waters. The reason it took a long for some of the adults in my relatives to adjust to Nia, was that she was the first Special Needs Child born into the family and secondly they wanted to understand her wants and needs.

When a young child first begins to express their wants to others outside their family there may be the need someone to translate for the child.

"What did the child say?"

"What does the child want?"

"Why is the child crying?"

"How come she does that?"

These are the types of things that are asked before language is clear enough to be understood without parental translation. In Nia's case, she was well into her teen years before those other than I could understand her needs without my constant translation. Once that occurred that "What does she want?" question was asked very infrequently because Nia would point to what she wanted, however, the "What did she say?" question would be around for many more years to come.

The introduction of different people in her life was good for Nia because it exposed her to people her age and older, and the behavior they exhibited. This became very clear while my entire family prepared for plays written, directed, and produced by my sister Debra.

Over a six-year period, my sister Debra wrote a series of plays, one of which was performed off-Broadway. I was a part of each play in one capacity or another and Nia was at every rehearsal. It was a total family effort and there was no one available to watch her during rehearsals. She had to sit and endure the retelling of lines time and time again, until she began to laugh where it was appropriate.

Nia grew up in front of all our eyes wanting to take part but not understanding how to join. Her eyes were riveted to the scene we rehearsed, her body language showed that she very much wanted to be a part of the play. One of the cast members Anna Dale made mention of Nia's clear entrance on the rehearsal stage.

"Next play we are going to need to find a scene for Nia" Ms. Anna said with a smile. It was a light moment but to me, it spoke volumes for where Nia was mental. She had grown in such a way that pushed far away from the lack of social connection making her more like teenagers her age. She wanted a connection and bringing her around others her age and not Special Needs may have diminished at least one aspect of being autistic. The acceptance of her cousin and the need to find what she wanted by the adults made Nia more sociable and more connected than most kids like her.

A THREE-RINGED CIRCUS

Talk to any parent of twins or stair-stepped children and they would explain the difficulty in dealing with multiple personalities at one time. Each child is its own individual and may develop differently depending on a whole host of factors. A parent who has their pulse of their children may very well deal with each child separately even though the same rule may have been broken. Each child deserves special moments with the parent all to themselves; when children feel another sibling is dominating the attentions adverse feelings come bubbling to the surface.

I did not have any children while Nia and I were growing comfortable with her disability. She had my total attention and I did not have to worry about the feelings of another child. If that sibling were as understanding as Jazmine there may be a good chance jealousy would not be an issue. If the sibling would have been like my twin nephews, then a schism could arise in the family if the questions turned into something more.

It is up to the parent to create an atmosphere where the needs of the Special Needs Child do not encroach upon the needs of the individuals in the family. The best atmosphere is one in which the disability is present but it does not become the conversation of each and every day.

I did not have that problem until much later in Nia's life. I could see how her disability could cause me to make choices that would have to be explained on a deeper level than just saying "because that is how things are." One has to do better than try to master raising a Special Needs Child alongside other children. One needs to be a master of a three-ringed circus, able to juggle multiple personality traits without forgetting the intended audience.

CHAPTER 18

On the average workday, I never liked to bring papers home to grade. My unofficial mentor at Martin Luther King Jr. High School, Lester Wallace, always spoke about "Working smart and not hard!" He was a strong proponent of leaving the work at school.

"There is no way I will bring this job home with me. It will bury you in a mountain of papers." His words were very true when it came to holiday breaks, there was no chance work would come home with me. For the first time in many years, I looked forward to having a real vacation. No Ni. No nieces. No nephews. Just what made me happy.

Nia's first stay at YAI went well enough that they called me several times including as a last-minute replacement. Her behavior at overnight was not exemplary but she was asked back again and again. Despite the spotty behavior, I was surprised when Nia was approved for a week's stay. She could adjust to anything; therefore, I was not worried in the least as to how she would react separated for one week. The concern for me was what the heck could I do for one week without having to think of the needs of Nia night and day.

The idea of spending one week away from Nia was set with anxiety and excitement for me. In nine years the only time I spent more than a weekend without Nia and it was me that needed to calm down and relax. Time off was greatly needed, nonetheless I needed to create a meaningful agenda to satisfy my desire to spend time away from Nia. Money was not a problem, finding something meaningful to occupy my time.

After dropping Nia off at YAI Friday night I took myself to the movies. It would be the first chance to see a movie without worrying about the time management. I went to see an action flick but what I viewed instead was a hybrid focusing on an unrealistic love story. The latter part made me think about my situation. Hell, all it took was the passing glance from any woman and my thoughts would turn to the blackness that was my love life. For a long stretch of time during the movie there was a period of self-examination I hoped would solve the riddle established by Jack Napier.

"If I were as good of a father as many women told me I was I would not be a three-time loser in love" I would say to myself in my darkest moments. Whenever those feelings were expressed in conversation with Killer he passed on a very famous statement about me using Nia as an excuse. Once again, I informed him that there were not many women who would take a man serious who was in his late thirties, and living with his mother while taking care of a child who would never move out of the house.

"The odds of finding a woman who could understand my situation were worse than the odds of hitting the lottery" I suggested to Killer.

"You never know what God has planned for you, Darryl" he reminded me. I understood his point but I may not be one of those people who would ever find love. For most of my adult life, I only had flashes of what a long-term love would mean in my life. Maybe Nia's mother was right when she made the following statement to me.

"You will never find anyone good because you treated me badly."

Her words proved to be prophetic. Since we parted, I could not hold a woman. No matter how many tried to convince me otherwise, there was no light in the darkness I felt.

Saturday afternoon I caught up with Cleve' at his work location to chat with him while he turned the lights on for about three hundred New Yorkers thrust into the dark through no fault of their own. We talked about the trip he and his longtime girlfriend took to Aruba two weeks prior. He spoke of the fun he had in the water despite the fact he cannot swim. As he spoke I remembered our long ago bet, and yet again he was the first between us to leave the country. After I left Cleveland I made my way down the street to see my Aunt Sylvia.

Sitting down for a warm chat with my aunt made me think about her in her younger years when she did her famous "Johnny Walker" dance. Her laugh was unmistakable and a joy to hear. It was my aunt who took care of Nia's mother when her ankles swelled after giving birth to our daughter. We laughed at the stories she told of the old days in our family. I left my Aunt that night and was glad that I spent the time with her. I headed home convinced that the rest of the week would be more fruitful.

Later that night I was in front of my television watching *Blaxploitation* Movies, as my mother relaxed on her couch after a long day at church. I sat at the edge of my bed as the former love of my childhood, Pam Grier performed in her classic movie "Foxy Brown." I wondered why there was not a woman like Pam in the world for me. Then I thought about the things Pam did to many of her men in her countless movies and my ideal woman transmuted to a safe Bernnadette Stains from Good Times. Too much Pam Grier can be a bad thing for a lonely man like myself, so instead of watching Pam kick ass, I watched Bernnadette's character Thelma tell J.J off.

Once under the covers, I stared up at the dark ceiling and thought back to the statement Nia's mother made. If I could undo the past I would undo most of my actions with her, but the only person who could forgive was not willing to see the way through his own deeds. The next day Sunday, I thought about going to church with my mother but I decided not to go after I looked into my closet to find no decent my lone suit and shoes would not qualify as my Sunday Best. Excuses were easy for me to make but the lack of money always played a big part in my failed dreams. Money was the root of all the evil in my life. My struggles are well documented but the emotions that go along with not having enough money ran the gamut from 'chagrin' to 'anger'. No matter the mood my lack of money was not improved. The moment I became a father I looked for ways to bring in more money to support my family. There was not an increased thirst for money, but if the opportunity arose would jump at the chance. In [the] education, there were many means to make money.

In order to increase my revenue stream coaching became my best means to make money. Nia limited what I could do and the hours I could work: but coaching was a pleasure for me. I also took converges, (Taking over one class for an absent teacher) to the degree that I was told to relax because some of my colleagues wanted some money too.

Each time a teacher is absent from school instead of paying a sub to work all day, a teacher's program could be divided among wanting teachers for Forty-four dollars each class. I did the math and if I did one each day I could bring in three hundred every three weeks. Once I became a Dean I could no longer do 'coverages', but I could coach more than one team. My quest for financial stability caused me to not see the importance of going to church. I always believed in God but evidently, I did not totally believe in the things he could do for me.

I had much to be thankful for, but there was that burning feeling that I should be doing more with my life. I had a good job but I had nothing more than bills to show for the hard work. I had a beautiful child but she was not "Normal." I had a roof over our heads but I lived with my mother. It seemed to me that everything I had was not enough. Maybe deep inside I thought I was not worthy of good because of what I had done to Nia's mother.

Instead of going to church, I chose to stay home to watch football until I turned blue in the face. As fate would have it both the New York teams the Jets, and the Giants were on television one after the other. During the halftime of the Jets game, my 860I Nextel began to tell me I had a call from Carlos Luisito Eugene Gonzales another close friend of mine. Perky, (as he was called from childhood) moved to Baltimore years earlier but we kept in touch. He worked as a salesman at a bedding store and for three years we talked on the phone Sunday afternoon. This particular Sunday as we talked over the phone, I decided I was going to make my first trip ever to visit him in Baltimore. Perky liked the idea and we set a date for that Wednesday for my trip. I finally would get out of the city and experience something new. The excuses of not having the time nor the money to do for myself were pushed aside, I was going regardless of what circumstances I would return to find at home.

Wednesday came fast enough to please my sense of adventure. I arose early in the morning to down my favorite breakfast of pancakes and bacon before my mother had to leave for church. I sat on the couch in usual silence and as well as loneliness. I did enjoy my moment but I had a feeling I was missing something.

CHAPTER 19

The last time I saw Perky, he showed up on the campus of Grambling State University in Louisiana. I exited the cafeteria and there he was standing arm in arm with one the sexiest girls on campus. I walked across the street to give him a homeboy hug for life. He drove the sexy woman down from Baltimore to attend classes, but he arrived for a heartwarming reunion. I did not know the next time I would see him years would pass between us.

After eating a great breakfast of pancakes and bacon prepared by my sweet mother, I made sure to wash the dishes we left in the sink. It was 9 AM in the morning and she already left the apartment for her doctor's appointments. I enjoyed the breakfast, but as I mentioned on occasion to my mother that she did not have to do as much as she did for Nia and for me. Her response was classic Rhoda Lawson. "Shut up! You have to learn how to accept a helping hand" she added. My mother told me she did not mind doing things for us and for Nia and me. I was slow to accept a helping hand extended to me from anyone. In my twisted mind asking for help would be an admission of failure. I could not easily accept help but I could offer help, which is why I did the little things around the apartment. I did things I believed my mother would like done and coming home to, vacuumed the rug and cleaned dishes, which is more than I ever did as a child living in the same apartment. As I stood in front of the door these thoughts passed through my mind as I prepared for my journey.

I locked the door to the apartment but I found my feet were unable to counter powerful gravitational forces. There was a strong fear that I had once more left something important inside the apartment. Immediately, I went through a mental checklist to ensure I had everything I wanted with me. No sooner than I exited the elevator I came in contact with Rahim, the building's longtime security guard. He knew everyone in the building as well as all their business to-boot. "I have a package for your mommy." Rahim was of Indian descent but he was raised on one of the Caribbean Islands. His keen eyes spotted the book bag I carried and he quickly took back his statement. "The package will keep. I don't want to interfere with your trip" he said as he waved his index finger in the air. "You deserve a break." "You're a great father" Rahim said as he returned to the security office. His departure allowed me to leave the building without further interruption. I left the building and into the cool morning air. I had been lucky to find a parking spot for my rental car right in front of the building after only twenty minutes of driving around the block. I looked west to 8th Avenue to see K.J. walking in the direction of the corner store. His appearance from afar looked as disheveled as our last encounter. I shook my head as I opened the car door and tossed my book bag into the car before K.J. saw me. It was 9 AM morning and already I had more than enough reasons to get away from the normal.

Once on the road, my regret for calling YAI to check on Nia was surpassed by the fact that I forgot most of the CD's needed for the three-hour drive to Maryland in my rental car. My limited music selection gave me the opportunity to think about how much I missed traveling. I had been in New York City for such a long time I truly had forgotten how the rest of the country looked.

Halfway down the venerable Interstate Highway 95, I glanced at the house that could be seen from just off the road and wondered, how different my life would have been had my father bought that house in New Jersey as he planned. Thinking about the past and what might have been was forbidden by my common sense, however my common sense could not win this battle.

The drive ignited a fire in me to make sure this would not be the last time I did for myself. Many times, I talked myself out of doing things that would make me happy. I didn't want to spend a dollar on fun today when I could pay a bill or buy food for the apartment. I believed in being practical but I was happy I did not listen to myself. The drive was easier than imagined because it had been a long time since the last time I drove a car longer than twenty minutes. My legs were cramped, and my back was very stiff however, the ride was worth every bit of the discomfort.

I called Perky for directions to his house and after many wrong turns and some backtracking, I finally arrived at my destination. The moment I peeled myself out of the car I gave him a huge brother hug. It had been years since I was able to embrace, my dear friends.

"Yo' man, you have to learn how to follow directions" he said to me with a laugh. Not one to be told how backward I could be at times, I defended myself by blaming his poor directions. We laughed at my lame attempt at deflection. It was good seeing him again instead of only hearing his voice over the phone. Seeing him again was enough to make me think about the block on which we both grew up.

CHAPTER 20

Perky and his older brother Michael were the first kids I met when I moved to 628 West 151st Street. Perky was the typical kid from Harlem, therefore, we shared many of the same things in common, while his older brother Michael could have been born to a family south of 110th Street. It was Michael who first introduced me to the music of The Rock, Gods Kiss, and Michael who was the first kid I knew that wanted to be a writer. I was close to Mike, but I could not get with the rock music or the huge comic book collection, plus Mike's age made me too young for him to hang out with while with Perky there was a little adjustment.

From our first meeting, we hit it off very well. He ate dinner at my apartment and I ate at his apartment as well. We played catch with the hardball and liked the same girl Flossy. Perky was the first person of Black and Puerto Rican descent I met. His nickname came from the fact that he could not sit still. As a child, he had a chunky build, which made him the brunt of the ubiquitous fat jokes to which he always had a strong comeback for the offending party. The adult who embraced me that day looked as if life had treated him very well.

The solid body of a man replaced his chunky kid body in his late thirties. The former record executive and business man, like all my friends still had most of the hair God granted. After our hug ended he walked me towards his door and a sense of joy came over me. I had not looked at the time in preparation for getting Nia off the bus. My mission to relax and free my mind had been completed. It was a good feeling that I did not want to end anytime soon.

He showed me around this city as if he were a tour guide. His knowledge of the city did not stop at locals he took me to eat the favorite food of most Baltimoreans, seafood! He took me to the historic Lexington Market where every type of seafood could be bought. I am not a big seafood fan but when in Baltimore do what Baltimoreans do. I ate soft-shell crab, raw oysters, and regular crab all for a reasonable price. As we dined our conversation turned to the events of our past and to the present.

"Where is Nia's mother?" Perky asked as we stood in front of a counter trying to decide what type of fish sandwich we should buy. He met her once while he came to visit me in my studio apartment. "She is down south living her life and leaving my life the hell alone." I half-joked as I settled on getting the classic Whiting sandwich. Perky decided on another type of fish then made a strong statement. "If I were you I would sue her for child support. If she had Nia she would not hesitate to take your money." Perky's suggestion was plausible but not practical for me. I did not want the aggravation of running to court in an attempt for getting "My Money" as most women would say. I did not want to take anything from her; instead, I wanted her to give from the heart. When I explained my rationale to him Perky could only shake his head. "You better think of them chicks and get your money!" Perky joked or so I thought. We ate the sandwiches we ordered and proceeded to walk toward the beautifully famous Inner Harbor. His suggesting of child support was not the first time I heard the suggestion, but it was the first time I heard it from a close male friend.

Living in New York City introduced me to the idea of living near water. Manhattan is surrounded by water but the odd fact is that most New Yorkers travel under or over the water and not on top of it like the people of Baltimore. There was a high level of activity on the water. I was amazed at how the city had kept a good part of its waterfront in good condition. Back home the Seaport in Lower Manhattan was the only place left with any type of bridge to New York's maritime past. Seeing history up close instead of reading about it in a dusty old book was enlightening.

The walk around Baltimore Harbor turned into a walk around the nearby mall. Perky wanted to show me one of his favorite stores in the mall. I long forgot the name of the store but I do remember that as the workers made chocolate candy they sang. Perky dropped some more history on me when he informed me that before R&B star Sisqo recorded his "Thong Song" he worked at that very store. In the middle of the song, my cell phone began to ring. I took it off my hip to realize the call came from YAI Respite.

The workers called me because Nia was acting out in the program. They wanted to know what I would do when she acted out. I could not tell them that I would bust her behind if she got out of line with me; I gave them the next best answer. "Take something away from her that she likes" I said as I tried to keep my cool. The worker said they would try to follow my suggestion. At the end of the conversation I hung up the phone and returned to my conversation with Perky, but it was clear that my thoughts were on Nia. "They get paid to deal with kids like her. They should not have to call you" Perky said as he guided me to a fancy diamond shop. He just met a new woman and he was thinking about getting married, and he wanted me to look at rings with him. Within twenty minutes of the last call, a second call came from YAI. According to the worker, Nia's behavior became more disruptive to the point they wanted her to leave.

When I informed them that I was not in town I could hear the frustration in their voice. There was no way I could get to her. I was of the mind that this was their job to handle my child. I hung up the phone with them and went back to looking at rings. Within a minute I was back on the phone this time with my mother.

I relayed what the worker at YAI told me and asked if she could get Nia. My mother was not the best at directions and she did not like riding the subway, and taking a bus would take time and the ability to find the building. She also was not dressed and it would take her sometime to get to Nia. A bus ride back home with an agitated Nia and luggage was not the best thing for either of them. YAI would have to wait until I arrived in New York to retrieve my child. Perky knew I was leaving Baltimore to drive back to New York and get Nia. He did not agree with me but he did not have to agree with me. I did not want Nia to be banned from the Respite Program. (Little did I know, that is just what happened.)

Perky took me back to my car. It was nearly four PM and I would not be able to get Nia until seven that night. I went against the philosophy of actor Eddie Murphy who once stated to Barbara Walters during an interview that having a Plan B was a plan to fail, and went to Plan B.

I called my ex-wife Taoussa, and asked her to get Nia from YAI then drop her off to my mother. She agreed and within seconds. I was on the phone with YAI to inform them that someone was on their way to get Nia sooner rather than later. I was able to coordinate this as a Maryland State Trooper issued my first ever speeding ticket. Twenty minutes after being ticketed I was on the road again driving just as fast as I kept an eye out for the police and on my rearview mirror.

My week vacation away from Nia turned into four-day respite. All mental gains of the week were exhaled due to the stress of the ticket as well as the entire rush to find someone to get Nia and get home to her. Everyone asked me why I never wanted to go on vacation this experience was the textbook reason why going away brought me stress.

I parked my rental car in front of the building and made my way upstairs. There was the usual crowd in front of the building doing what the people of *310* did year-round. Upon my entry Rahim was long gone, Monroe replaced him as the Security Guard. He worked in the building as long as Rahim did and was just as friendly.

Monroe and I had long talks about sports, which sometimes delayed my getting upstairs although I knew how slow the elevators were in the building. I was in a rush to get upstairs and see Nia but Monroe did manage to have me miss the elevator.

"A pretty young lady dropped Nia off about an hour and a half ago" he said in his rich southern accent. I felt relief that she was upstairs and started to relax just a little. I thanked Monroe and luckily caught the next elevator, which brought a large amount of people down to the lobby. The instant I put the key in the door I could hear Nia let out a yell. I walked into the apartment to see a big smile on Nia's face. Her mental clock was set for spending two days away from me and not four. "She has been looking out of the living room window for you" my mother informed. The living room window looked to the back of the building and on occasion, I would enter the building from the back. I could not be mad at her but I was upset that her behavior cut short my vacation. I gave her a hug then checked in with my mother before going into my room and calling my Taoussa to thank her for her much needed help, and Perky to let him know I made it home safely but a few dollars short.

The trip to see Perky was a fun experience, which reminded me of how I put restrictions on myself. Nia was my alpha and my omega of each day, and I better understand in order to adjust my life around her life. Sometimes we have to protect our child from their own actions: but most of the time we have to protect them from others.

CHAPTER 21

I stood on the corner checking my watch as I looked up and down the avenue for the bus carrying Nia. My heart jumped out my chest as I thought the call made by Christine informing me that Nia's bus had not arrived at the after-school program. Christine was a Paraprofessional at Nia's school, who took a special liking to Nia. When she called me on the phone Nia's bus was already one hour late. Christine called the bus company twice, and I called the Office of Pupil Transportation three times and no one could tell me where the hell my child was.

There were only two instances in my life that I was ready and willing to lose full control; this was the second such occasion. My child was on a school bus with two strangers for one hour and she would not be able to tell me what happened. My greatest fear of raising Nia was something would happen to her and she would not be able to speak for herself. The worst possible thoughts came to mind about what could have happened to my daughter.

I placed another call to the bus company and in not so kind words let it be known that my child better appear unharmed and in a hurry. The operator made matters worse when she said the driver was not answering the two-way radio. I was about to really lose my mind on the unfortunate operator when I received a call from Christine. I rudely ended my call with the operator to take Christine's call. Christine let me know Nia arrived at the after school program just in time to be taken off one bus and be placed on the bus that would her home.

"Where was she?" I asked Christine as my anger over the phone. My anger was represented by spittle flying out of my mouth as I spoke.

"They said they dropped off other kids before they brought her to the after school" she responded. Her words contradicted what I had been told. "That's bull Christine. The bus dispatcher just told me, that the driver told her, the after school was closed." I started to shout but I remembered who I was talking to and brought my volume down. As my volume went down my words caused Christine to raise her volume. "I stood outside for almost an hour. That's a freaking lie Darryl, I stood outside for an hour" Christine bluntly stated. She did not have to tell me what to do next. I wanted to find the driver and matron and choke the life out of them. I did not know where they took my daughter for a two hour *joyride* but I wanted very much to have an audience with them to find out.

When Nia's bus arrived, she seemed normal which relieved some of my stress. She was tired therefore I rushed her upstairs to my mother who was just as angry as I. The very next day I filed a complaint with the city. I was not about to let anyone get away with taking advantage of my child. Once I conversed with my sister Debra I took Nia to the doctor to make sure no one had done something foul to her. Lord, help me if they did.

The hardest thing I had to do up to that period of time was to take my child to the hospital and explain to the doctor that I wanted her checked to see if my child was sexually abused. There was nothing I could do but wait for the results. The exam could not take place because Nia fought the doctor at every point of the potential exam: so much so, the doctor had to stop.

"If she is fighting me this hard then we can argue that nothing happened to her" the doctor said as she removed her rubber gloves and tossed them into the garbage. My state of mind was such that I took her words as the truth I could not prove. With my fear somewhat calmed I turned my attention and anger towards the driver and the bus matron. I placed several calls to the Office of Pupil Transportation concerning the status of the investigation on where the male driver and male matron took my daughter for an hour with no response. Since the rich guy became mayor of New York City in 2002, OPT turned into the most dysfunctional branch of the Department of Education I knew. Yes, they had to bus more kids in a day than the populations of some American cities, but the manner in which they operated was ass-backwards. To ignore the calls of a concerned parent spoke volumes about how the office viewed the fragile individuals they transported.

During a quiet lunch period, I decided to give OPT one more chance. To my surprise, the supposed director of the investigation unit answered my call. I hoped to get some answers to my questions but the woman became the third person in my life I wanted to kill. The woman's attitude toward me was how her office treated all parents who called the office for help. Instead of lending a sympathetic ear to a highly agitated parent, the woman chose to try to cover her ass in an attempt to make me out to be a fool. Upon asking the sorry excuse for a woman if she received any of my messages, she chose to call me a liar in a roundabout but obvious way.

With me still, on the phone, the woman pulled the phone away from her ear to inhumanly call out to her secretary if they (Her office) had received any of my calls. I could not believe she was trying to deflect the reason of my calls, trying to shake my focus. The SOB had another thing coming.

"Are you calling me a liar?" I yelled over the phone. The woman stopped calling to her secretary to speak to me.

"You did not call this office sir" she said in a dismissive tone of voice. I was in the teacher's cafeteria at the time I made the call and there were people present; but I did not care who might have been there, I was not about to take being called a liar.

"If I didn't call, it doesn't flipping matter, I am calling you now. What are you going to do about the driver and the matron?"

My voice was full of anger and my heart pounded in my chest hard enough that I could feel veins pop out of my forehead. The woman continued to infer that if she did not call then there was no problem. "Check this out I will be to your office within the hour." "Make sure you keep your nasty ass attitude when you see me in person." I meant every word I said to her then I hung up my phone. I was hot and that chick who called me a liar was about to understand my concerns. I stormed out of the Teacher's Cafeteria on the fifth floor and headed to the main office on the first floor. It was in the middle of the day, yet I was leaving work to deal with my situation. The principal had given teachers trouble about leaving work early: but if he denied my exit I would leave anyway.

I met the Assistant Principal in the hallway and let him know that I was leaving no matter what, and he gave no resistance. The crazed look in my eyes must have convinced him to just let me go. I signed myself out of work and was on the train to Queens within ten minutes from hanging up the phone. As I traveled to my confrontation I ran over multiple scenarios in my mind to how I would react if the woman did not give me the answers I demanded. My anger got the best of me, because all of the scenarios took a dark turn.

I reached the building on Vernon Avenue in Long Island City Queens and I was deviously calm. If I entered the building with an attitude I would have alerted The School Safety Officer stationed at the door that I was up to no good. Calmly I asked for the woman and signed the guest book and made my way to OPT.

Upon announcing my presence, I was told to take a seat and wait for the woman. I took the seat knowing full well that this was one technique to calm an irate parent down. Some time passed by before an older white man emerged from the office instead of the woman I very much wanted to see. This was the second technique to calm a parent down, deny them the source of the anger. The older white man spoke in a voice of a museum curator discussing a piece from the Bronze Age. I continued to look over the man's shoulder at the door he emerged from, hoping that my offender would show her face.

"I can tell you, Mr. Lawson, that we have investigated and have suspended both the driver and the matron" he old man said as he read from a folder that could have held the day's junk mail. I never thought of asking for a copy of the report. Instead, I kept looking for that chick to come out the door and continue to call me a liar. My anger blocked my judgment. I should have asked for a copy of the report which would have been total proof that the older white man was not a liar himself. I chose to take the man's word and left the office knowing full well I had just had my job saved for me. From that day forward my lasting opinion of OPT is more than I could place on this page.

CHAPTER 22

Since I was a child my family has always spent time together. Holidays, birthdays, special occasions we were together. I loved having my family around because each relative was unique in personality. The events I enjoyed more than birthday cake and Ice cream were the family bus rides. It seemed every summer we rented a bus and headed for one of the many amusement parks in the Tri-State area. Those trips built memories and were precious, but with all good things the bus trips came to an end. For several years we did nothing during the summer but the year Nia was born my family booked a weekend trip to Virginia Beach, Virginia.

Nia was too young to take on the long bus ride. I watched sadly as the bus pulled away from in front of me, but I was happy not be alone. I had my daughter and her mother which made being left behind acceptable. Several months later, I left my relatives behind and drove my family to South Carolina to visits her mother's side of the family. It was the only time Nia and I would ever see them.

When Nia was around six years old members of my family rented vans and drove south for a vacation to Myrtle Beach South Carolina. South Carolina is where Nia's mother was born and raised and where her family lived. During this period of time, her mother and I had sporadic communications, plus my attitude towards her had not softened. I was not sure how her mother would react when it was time to leave, therefore I did not attempt to contact her. The next time we traveled south, I made it a point to let her mother know.

The second trip to Virginia Beach saw Nia and I participate. We spent a weekend in the water or shall I say Nia spent the weekend frolicking in the Atlantic Ocean. I can still see her jumping in the waves without fear. She became comfortable enough to move further out in the surf which was very dangerous. I maintain a healthy fear of water and was fearful to go in the ocean above my knees. Nia went that far out and for a moment I froze. My cousin Joanna was an excellent swimmer, went out after Nia. I lost my fearless father card that day. On the way back to the city we visited the Six Flags Amusement Park. Nia's mother lived in Richmond and I gave her a call to set up a meeting when we were at the park. The sound of her mother's voice made me feel sure that Nia would get the chance to see her mother for the first time in years.

My time in the park was very enjoyable but I had one eye and one ear on my phone waiting for Nia's mother to call. I continued to hold out hope, peering out the window of the bus to catch a glimpse of her. Hope faded once the bus pulled out for New York without one word from her. In that moment I gave up any and all hope. I knew Nia's mother was never going to see her child again. She later told me that she was unexpectedly called back to work and was unable to call me. Her excuses were plausible but it did not do anything for Nia. My curiosity about how Nia would react to seeing her mother once again was not strong enough to extend my hand again.

The next trip Nia and I took was to Sin City Las Vegas. Fifty of my family members were on the same plane hurtling across the country to the city envisioned by New York Jewish Mobster Benjamin Siegel. On the flight out to Vegas I counted all the money I would make gambling and all the fun I would have winning my riches. My fantasy was interrupted by Nia who had trouble with her ears.

For most of the flight west Nia placed her fingers in her ears. I assumed her ears popped. After I gave her a stick of gum to chew on Nia began to feel like herself. Taking care of Nia was what I did. Our stay at a kid friendly hotel was a great idea. All the kids that came with us lived in the pool by the day. We chose to go in August the hottest month possible and the pool was a good choice. I did not have to fear the strong ocean waves knocking me down, therefore I followed Nia around the pool making sure she did not swallow too much water. The temperature was in the high 90's but Nia stayed in the water until she shivered as if it were winter time. I had a great time but Nia had a better time hanging out in the pool of the hotel, it gave me the opportunity to bond with her on another level.

As the sun began to set, spending time with Nia took a backseat to gambling. There are two good reasons to visit Las Vegas and one of them I could not do on this family excursion. I lined up my bills in perfect order in dominations from one to fifty. I wanted to stack the money in such a way that I would appear to be a high roller and not a sucker to be taken. Nia sat on the bed watching me and despite my warning, I returned from the bathroom to find my gambling money all over the floor. I restacked the bills and began to dial the rooms for someone to watch Nia while I went gambling. It was my horror to realize everyone who could go had gone gambling leaving me out in the cold in the desert. I put my money back in my wallet and went to sleep. I did have a great time, but the fact that I spent most of the four days with only Nia made me think of my old theme. All she knew was her father, which I feared that she was getting too attached to me and she needed a female in her life. My thoughts got me to thinking about her mother. All the other kids in the family knew their mother intimately except my child.

My curiosity got the better of me. The next time I spoke to Nia's mother, I made sure to mention that it had been five years since Nia saw her and that she had to give her child the opportunity to see her once more. Her mother was not keen on my suggestion but I let her know the next time we made arrangements to meet I was coming no matter what she said. Her mother told me she understood how serious I was and she could not disappoint her child ever again.

The next vacation I would take would be one to unite my child with her mother just for that moment. I thought for a moment how Nia had been up and down the East Coast and on a plane to Las Vegas at an early age. She was an experienced traveler on the New York Subway System and she had been all over the city. Yes, we traveled in all types of weather that should have kept us in the house. The one trip I wanted her to take was out of my control.

Not That Type of Connection

I did not shield Nia from the world as much as my instincts told me I should. Every parent wants to protect their child from harm and I was no different. Her condition would have made it easy to hold her tight, to make less demands of her. Treating her as if she were not capable of doing more each day would have truly retarded her emotional and mental growth.

There are some drawbacks to taking Nia out in the world, like I soon realized that Nia did not like loud noises, therefore, concert and parties were not always the best place to take her. The more she was around noises the stronger her endurance became for them. Sticking her fingers in her ears and humming was her signal that there was too much noise in her environment, which I found odd because she would blast music in the house over the computer.

When in the house Nia could be counted on to dominate the television. Having any child sit in front of the idiot box for prolonged periods of time was not the best way to consume time. Nia would watch games shows, like her beloved wheel of Fortune and Lingo. She would watch Barney and my favorite Sesame Street. Once she learned how to use the computer she would listen to music and view pictures from our past. Later when YouTube came into our lives she would watch episodes of Barney, Wheel, and Martin. Whatever she watched as a child she found on YouTube. I was amazed that after showing her how to get on the web Nia ran with it.

Some would say it was a good thing that she could occupy her time on the computer, but just like too much television is bad too much computer is equally bad. Nia would grow leaps and bounds: but I still and always wonder how much more she would have grown if her mother never left.

CHAPTER 23

I became very adept at playing the game of charades as a single father. I did not want anyone to worry about me, therefore I kept my emotions to myself. My lows were hidden from sight by elaborate distractions of telling everyone that I was fine. As told earlier, I had the tendency to suffer bouts of self-doubt and lack of confidence. I tricked myself into believing I had a good handle on my emotions: but every so often the weight on my shoulders took me to a place of total reflection.

Once again, we were back on the beach in Virginia when Nia ran head first into the Atlantic. This time I did not panic and allow my cousin to save Nia, I unflinchingly ran toward the knee high waves to save my baby. Suddenly the reason for my fear of water came into the thought. I saw myself underwater again. I quickly took my head out from the shower as I felt very uncomfortable. My incident in the water brought me to another unfortunate situation.

My vivid imagination took me back to my time in Family Court. As I stood waiting for my name to be called, I watched two parents use their child in a game of, "Go tell your…" Back and forth he went about his task unaware he was being mistreated by those he loved. Seeing how those parents acted, gave me just one more minute of pause. I didn't want Nia to be put in a position where I could not help her. My shower was longer than usual and for once I was happy not to live in a home and pay a water bill. My memory chain turned into more like a daisy chain, and thoughts kept coming.

The voice of my cousin David drowned out the sounds of the water hitting my body.

"Man stop complaining and do something about your situation" he demanded. His Uncle Charles Anthony, put it another way:

"Weight broke the wagon." I was sent back to the time I did not have enough money to buy an Ice Cream cone for Nia when that was what she said she wanted, and there were some of the few words she could say. The feeling I had the instant I knew my pockets were empty was probably my lowest moment as a provider.

"Did I do anything right'?"

I did not have an answer for my question, God knew. I just had to find the solution. Nia and I had come along way, and we had a longer way to go. After allocating an enormous amount of time to putting out fires and dealing with unknown issues that would arise, I had a moment.

In the middle of a long shower I suddenly broke down in tears. I hated to cry, not because it is not seen as a manly thing to do: but because for me crying meant I had reached a crossroads. I was overcome by rolling emotions that would not come to rest easily in the shower. I had come to the point in my thinking that I was the personification of Langston Hughes' poem, "Dream Deferred." It seemed I was happy, but not happy enough, with how my life was progressing. I had Nia but there had to be more. More for me to do with Nia, and without her. My cry ended when once again I convinced myself once again, failure was not an option.

I felt trapped in a life that was the one I now lived. It was always my impression that I could have done more but somehow more was not forthcoming. My life could best be summed up as incomplete. I had a job but nothing really to show for my hard work. I had a beautiful child, who could not wish me a good morning. I had a heart that ached to be given to someone, but that someone was a description in my mind. I had many skills but none of which were sufficient enough to give me that sense of fulfillment I longed craved. Finally, good thoughts came to mind.

Nia's mother was a bridesmaid in a wedding in which I was a groom. The wedding was taped and the tape, yes, I said the tape was given to us as a present. Nia learned how to use the VCR on her own. Waking her up in the morning was a difficult endeavor for me and getting her to stay still long enough for me to take a rare nap was also difficult. I learned early on that music videos were the solution to each problem. When normal means to wake a child proved ineffective, I would place a tape of videos I made and Nia would spring to life. Whenever I need to take a nap Nia would sit quietly long enough to allow me to rest my tired body. It was not long before she learned how to put the tapes in the VCR on her own to watch the videos. The wedding tape began to be part of viewing habits and taught me about Nia.

Nia would play the wedding tape and rewind each time her mother would appear. She did not say anything but her eyes would be as wide as her mother's each time she saw her image. Nia eventually focused in on one scene where her mother was announced and escorted into the hall. She rewound the scene until that part of the tape became warped. My daughter showed me that Autism had not severed her feelings from those she loved. The video was one means but music became another.

Music is everything for me. I love music for music is the key to my soul. My love was transferred to Nia. She learned how to put a CD into the CD player and that was all she wrote. Mary J Blige became the early morning wake up call for me. Each morning she would get out of bed and place the same CD into the player and belt out the same song. I guess she taught me like I taught her. She found a Brian McKnight CD, which she liked, and one song that would bring her to tears. Whenever it played just before it ended Nia would be in tears. The song happened to be part of the wedding video and the logical conclusion was that it reminded her of her mother. She was still in love with her mother.

When we moved in with my mother, the music fetish was still present but she stopped watching the wedding video. The tape was somehow lost during the several moves we made and Nia's sympathetic tears ceased to fall. Autistic children were supposed to be detached from the world, but Nia proved that she was very much aware of her place in it and whom she loved. I was happy at the amount of growth she made, but was I ready to grow myself was still open.

I should have known better to control my issue of self-worth because I was a teacher of history, and there were many stories of individuals who looked at what might have been instead of enjoying what was. I could have followed the teachings of Buddha who told "That unfulfilled desires bring unneeded disappointments." I could see the point, but to live without wants in America would be difficult. I could have also followed the examples of Christ who told his followers that "The gate to heaven is a narrow one but the gate to hell is very wide." Desire for me was the widest road to hell. My wanting and not achieving had made me see life as it should be and not how it was for me. I had still not yet understood the cause of my feelings; and it would take the simple words of a car commercial to bring that idea home.

There was a good basketball game on cable. I was tired of seeing the Knicks blow games they should win and win games they could have lost. My mother joked that the Knicks coach at the time Van "Grumpy" as he was affectionately called, had lost his hair because of the erratic play of his team. I thought it was a funny statement but watching them was frustrating for real. They had more talent than most teams, but their talent could not overcome their miscues as well as the plots Die Hard Knicks Fans swore were hatched against them. Right after Coach Van Grumpy called a late time out, I did not leave for a bathroom break choosing to lament about a possible ugly loss by my favorite team.

A Mazda car commercial aired during the game. The simple hook in the commercial defined happiness as enjoying what you already have. It was a simple but effective pitch. I could not afford a car at the time but the more I saw the commercial the more I began to formulate my own idea of what happiness was and in time I realized how blind I had been.

The focus of my life was on me and not on Nia. What I came to realize was what Nia wanted she already had in her life. If I was not focused on me I would have been able to focus more on her and her needs, not my desires. Up to that point in my life, I looked forward to where I wanted to be and not where I stood. I should enjoy what I already had because there was no chance I would appreciate whatever we were able to gain. It was then that I grew as a man and as a father. My down moments no longer were filled with tears; they were filled with hopes and fewer desires and less fear.

REFLECTION

The older Nia became the more she began to look and act like her mother. Whenever she was scared her eyes would widen just like her mother. If she were sad her facial expressions would take me back to her mother as well. There were many similarities between the two, more than I hoped.

It was a strange thing about my family, it seemed that most of us held similar appearances. Some say Nia looked like my cousin Alenda, others continued to say she looked just like me. My mother and my sisters said I had many characteristics of my long-deceased father, from my looks and mannerisms right down to my love of history all came from him. Thinking about my father caused me to pause in thought about how much Nia remembered about her mother.

How much did she remember of the four years they spent together? Did Nia remember how she called out her mother's full name when she was just six months old? Did Nia recall playing with her long black hair or how Nia would get her mother to stroke her long nails along her arms? Could Nia recall the loud fights and arguments that took place between her immature parents? There was a plethora of things I wondered about how much Nia could remember about her life. I often asked her in hopes that one-day she would respond in a manner that would let me know her mind was capable of memory recall.

Nia was not yet a teenager but she already could express her feelings with attitude and demands. Nia even made the mistake of storming away from me and slamming her room door behind her. She acted like a normal teenager and I responded like a normal parent would when a child stormed off and slammed doors in a house the child did not pay rent.

She acted more like a regular pre-teenager than I would ever imagine Nia would. In spite of her growth, there was something missing there was something more she needed that I could not give my daughter. I felt she needed a mother or at the least a mother's love. I became more determined to find a way to reunite her with her mother. Only then did I feel Nia had a good chance of showing me how much she had grown. There were times in my profession that I did not have the opportunity to experience the growth of my students, sometimes they came to me having acted like an adult.

CHAPTER 25

For the second day in a row, I received a new student in the class. It was unusual for this to happen and it had happened twice in the same week and late in the school year. The first student came to our school on a safety transfer meaning there was a safety issue at the student's last school. It was clear from the blank expression on the young girl's face that she was not the perpetrator but most likely the victim. The second student transfer had an expression that was very intriguing.

We were not supposed to ask students why they transferred to our school because of the sensitive nature of the incident that may have caused the safety transfer. Being a Dean gave me advantages regular teachers did not because one of the Deans had to input the student's data on the computer in order for the student to have an identification card. I did not have the opportunity to ask Dean Shorts, how the young man came to our school; therefore, it took me a few days to pry the information out of the student.

The young man had a serious way about him but at the same time, he seemed very, very unusual for someone his age. Many of his mannerisms reminded me of a young person who had been around too many adults. He could have had older male relatives or he could have been hanging out with older men in his neighborhood. He stayed to himself most of the time in class doing work but he participated in few class discussions. Other times he acted like the rest of his classmates snapping jokes and acting goofy. His actions were out of the ordinary, which only served to spark my curiosity. Either case, I wanted to know his story in order to deal with him in the least restrictive manner. My opportunity to speak with him outside the class came during a chance meeting in the hallway.

As I patrolled the halls I came upon said student well after the late bell. He saw me and knew the question of his repeated absence to my class was going to be brought up in conversation.

"Your attendance has been spotty lately." What happened to you?" I asked as I approached him in a non-threatening manner. His perfect attendance quickly turned spotty just two months after his arrival. I could have made a big deal about him being in the halls and not in class but that approach would have caused him to react in a defensive manner. The young man looked me straight in my eyes as he gave his answer.

"I had some things I had to do" he responded sheepishly. The way the young man answered my open-ended question led me to believe that he was a tough kid. No matter what the conversation I have with students I always found a way to swing it back to the lesson at hand or about the importance of school.

"You can't come and go like the wind and expect to graduate on time."

I shot back as I checked the hallway for other stragglers. I then tried to use his words as a vehicle of understanding for him.

"What was your attendance like in the school you were in last year?" I asked. His answer would fill in some of the story for me. There was no way I could have expected his frank response.

"I was in jail in Ohio all last year. I never missed one day there!" he laughed. The young man paused for a moment as he probably contemplated about telling me the reason for his incarceration, but soon he told me the entire story before I could tell him the reason was none of my business.

"My mother's husband was beating her bloody, I had to save her so I hit him with a bat. The mother fucker stopped hitting her. He stopped breathing too." He spoke in a matter of fact voice as if he had come to reconcile his actions and the impact it would have on his life a long time ago. I was speechless for a few seconds. Attending school every day seemed to pale in comparison to going to jail for murder at 16 years of age. The young man made an adult decision that brought along with it adult consequences.

My silence lasted just as long as it took for me to bring the conversation back to the importance of a high school graduation. "You had to make a choice then to save your mother's life, and now you have to make a decision to save your own life by getting an education. Bring your ass to class." I wanted to end the conversation on an educational note. The young man shook his head in agreement with me about taking care of business in school, I gave him dap and escorted him into his nearby class as his living excuse. As I resumed my patrol my thoughts were with the adult decision the young man had to make. He had to kill a man to protect his mother from her mistake of choosing the wrong man. My reaction was not as an educator but rather as a man raised in New York City.

I did not have disdain for the young boys' actions. If one had to kill then the protection of one's mother should be on the top of that list. It does not make it right but I fully understood the decision he made that fateful day. Graduating from Humanities High School should be his main goal but there were so many things he had to deal with in addition to gaining a formal education.

After that meeting, I never saw the young man again in or around the school building. Through the years I wondered what had become of him but I will probably never know. How the young man saved his mother's life was a total opposite of how many students felt about their mothers.

To my surprise, there were many students over my years of teaching that openly stated a dislike for the person that pushed them into this world of sin. I have forgotten the reasons for the dislike long ago, however it always amazed me to know that some mother, child relationships were more volatile than that of Republicans and Tea Party Republicans. What could cause such dysfunction in what should be one of the most pristine relationships known to man is too voluminous to fathom. My child had not seen her mother at that point for five years. There was a side of me that hoped that Nia had not grown to dislike her mother as many of my students had professed about their mothers. The other side, let's not go there.

My experiences at work forced me to make up my mind about taking Nia to see her mother. The telephone calls were not enough because Nia would not spend more than a few seconds on the phone and be off to finish watching Barney. She had to see her mother, and I had to see her too: to start the process of mending fences.

CHAPTER 26

I was a grown man with a child and bills to pay but still there was a part of me that was not sure all the decisions I made were good ones. I needed to get some feedback from family and friends to make sure faulty logic was not used in my decision to take Nia south to see her mother. The idea did not sit well with many.

"What the shit is this Darryl?" my Aunt Joyce said to me when I informed her that I was about to take Nia to see her mother for the first time in six years. "She may try to run off with Nia. You be careful" my aunt added. She was very serious in reaction to my news. I broke the news to my family as we sat at my aunt's house celebrating something or another. I chose that moment because I would get raw and immediate, unfiltered discourse. I watched the expression on my mother's face immediately change from festive to downright angry. If she weren't of a dark complexion I would assume she would have turned beet red in the face.

"She better not try anything crazy. I'll go down there and kick her ass" my mother rambled off. Whenever she was agitated my mother spoke with enough animation that could not be emulated. My mother's animations aside, the reactions of the rest of the revelers had strong reservations about my decision. All they wanted to know was if I would allow her to take Nia anywhere without me.

"I will not let that girl out of my sight" I assured the gathering. I too had doubts but my doubts centered on would there be any parting hysterics on the part of her mother when it was time to leave? Or would Nia cry like she did when her mother would leave her in the house with me as she went to the store? I was sure of nothing more than I would have to find out.

The closer the date came for us to leave the more confident I became in my decision. In preparation for the first face-to-face meeting with her mother, I spoke to Nia about the proposed trip as I had done the first time I took her to *Respite*.

"We will soon go to see your mother Nia" I repeated to her. In typical Nia fashion, she repeated the last word I said. I was not sure if she fully understood me but nonetheless, I had to explain the situation to Nia. The morning we were set to leave I felt no apprehension. Not even after I received last-minute calls from Debra and Jackie did I feel that I made a bad move. I loaded up the rental car with CD's, I remembered to bring along and snacks for the five-hour ride to her mother; the sound of joy in her mother's voice as we made final arrangement gave no hint of any trouble.

The last time I went a long car ride with Nia she was about two years old. Her mother and I drove her down south to see her great-grandmother among others. The drive took twelve hours and I did all the driving. I wanted to test myself and I passed the test but yet failed the class because when I found myself asleep at Nia's great-grandmother's house I woke up several times through the night still thinking I was driving. On the way back to New York I let her mother start out and I took the wheel several hours later. This time Nia was not a cute little girl sitting in a car seat quietly staring out of the window. Nia was much older and much more aware of her surroundings.

I made the mistake of leaving around noon, which meant that I would run into traffic around the Nation's Capital. My brother-in-law Curtis warned me of the impending doom I was to meet, but I decided to leave around Noon anyhow. Prior to hitting D.C. traffic, I hit a more sinister obstacle, one that caused me to talk to myself for one-half hour.

Like a flash, I began to worry about what would I do if I had to go to the bathroom and Nia did not? There was always an uncomfortable situation with me taking Nia into a bathroom when I had to go. I was always careful that during our long train rides through the city we would be home by 6PM. It seemed that time was her scheduled time to use the bathroom. The one time I could remember not making it home by that time my baby wet herself my saving grace was that it happened to be raining that day thus Nia was saved from embarrassment. There was no way she could be saved if the episode arose while we were in the car.

As I drove down I-95 I thought back to what my cousin Charles told me about his own experience. He told me that he pulled into a McDonalds and took over the bathroom, which allowed him and his granddaughter to use the bathroom alone. Four hours into the drive I found a McDonalds and took over the bathroom and my mind relaxed. My relaxation lasted until I hit traffic just outside of the Nation's Capital.

It was just passed six and Nia told me through sign language that she had to use the bathroom. I pulled over onto the grass shoulder of the road and tried to have her use the bathroom by the road but Nia clearly told me "No." I took heed and got back into the car and prayed that the traffic would soon clear and we could make it to our destination without any accidents.

We arrived at our motel sometime after 7 p.m. just in time for Nia to run into the bathroom. I was tired from the drive but my adrenaline was flowing. He mother called me for the fourth time just as I pulled into the parking lot of the motel and within fifteen minutes there was a knock on the door. There was no hesitation about me opening the door for I was ready to get the long-drawn-out act over. I made my way over to the door, held my breath and opened it.

CHAPTER 27

"Hey, Deryl" Nia's mother said as she as she entered the room. She always pronounced my name with a southern drawl. I stepped aside as she rushed past me. It was clear she did not want to see me as much as she wanted to see her child. From the quick glance I got from the fast-moving blur, Nia's mother looked the same as she did the last time I had seen her in the flesh. Her hair was still long with no trace of gray and her strong accent had not softened.

"Well, hello to you" I said closing the door behind her. She stood next to the bed surveying the room when I closed the door I walked over to her and gave her the answer to the question she wanted.

"She is in there" I said as I pointed to the bathroom as the sound of the flushing toilet gave away Nia's whereabouts. Nia's mother waited patiently for her child to emerge from the bathroom. Nia exited the bathroom and stood in shock at the sight of her mother.

"Hey, Nia. How are you doing?" her mother asked as she kept her distance from her child. I was surprised that Nia's mother did not run over to give her child a huge hug. If that had been me who had spent six years away from my child, I would have squeezed the stuffing out of her. I did not ask why but I can only assume that her actions were a combination of events of our past.

For too long I did not care what Nia's mother felt about the life we shared in common. If she ever saw Nia again I would not have lost any sleep: but once again it would come to me much later that Nia's feeling should have been my main concern. Being a parent meant that I was partly responsible for a life and because of that fact I needed to do what was best for her, which may not be good for me.

Like always Nia repeated the last word her mother said to her. Since Nia's speech was not easily understood her mother did not understand what her child said. This would not be the last time that weekend I served as an interpreter.

"She is so pretty" her mother proudly confessed but in the next sentence, she repeated her usual head-scratching statement.

"Nia looks nothing like me" she said with all seriousness. Her comment took me back to the time while on the operating room table she complained about Nia being born a girl and not a boy. I wanted to set her straight then just as I wanted to set her straight again.

"I don't understand you. She looks exactly like you" I said to counter her bogus claim. Nia's Mother did not put up much resistance she probably knew the obvious. Nia laughed and smiled for a moment then she moved over to the television to cut it on. Nia's mother did not know what to think of her daughter paying only a fleeting interest in her. I interceded to let Nia's mother know her child's action was not personal.

"She usually watches Wheel of Fortune at this time" I informed. Her mother could not believe that her child still watched Wheel of Fortune.

"You remember she used to call out the letter "T" during Wheel of Fortune?" her mother shouted in amazement. Nia turned to her mother and once again called out the same letter to which I needed to translate. There were a few minutes of awkward conversation mostly centered on the places and things we shared in the past. I changed the topic when my stomach began to grumble.

"What does she like to eat?" her mother asked me. Her question gave me an opportunity to have her mother bond with her child.

"She can answer you. Just ask her" I said as a reminder that Nia could talk. Her mother took my advice and asked Nia what she wanted to eat, and Nia gave her mother an answer even though I had to translate it gave her mother a chance to speak directly to Nia and get a response. Nia, let it be known that she wanted to eat McDonald's because she repeated her word for McDonalds as she pointed to her mother's chest then to her own. It was Nia's way of telling her mother to take her to McDonald's.

"There is one just down the road. I will take you two there" her mother said as she flashed her familiar smile and much to Nia's delight drove us to McDonald's.

One of the reasons Nia's mother gave for not seeing her daughter years earlier was that she claimed that Nia would not know her anymore. Nia would have forgotten she ever existed. Her mother's assumption was just as incorrect as the one she had about Nia's looks. As I stood on line ordering food I looked back at Nia interacting with her mother. It took me back to the time we all lived under the same roof. There were some good memories for me sandwiched between times I would do best to disremember. Seeing those two together once again made me contemplate all the distance that had existed between them causing the daughter to try to remember what it was like to have a mother and the mother trying to forget what it was like not to have been in Nia's life.

In that moment I wished for a way to erase the past and replace it with only positive memories. There would be no miracles forthcoming, my past would remain with me forever. The joy on the face of her mother hid many questions. I kept my thoughts to myself as I interrupted the joyous reunion when I brought the food to the table. Nia was happier than I had seen her in a long time. The moment in McDonald's was worth the trip south.

After dinner, Nia's mother drove us back to the motel. She did not leave right away instead Nia's mother gave Nia a bath for old times' sake. From outside the bathroom door, I could hear Nia hum in a way that showed she was happy. My time alone in the room gave me time to think about all that I went through with the woman behind the bathroom door that caused me to deflect comments from people who complimented me on my stewardship over Nia.

I had allowed someone's actions to tarnish my own view of myself. I was not in the area code of going to church, therefore, I had no idea that until I forgave myself then I would not seek the forgiveness of the person I hurt. It would take several years before we had a real conversation about the things we did to one another that brought both of us out of character. No one could have told either of us our lives would have turned out like they did, separate and awkward.

Nia emerged from the bathroom draped in a towel thus I had to pull myself out of the thoughts of the past to deal. Her happy face made my former soft feelings disappear in favor of the stoic countenance of a Roman Patrician. By the time her mother entered the room my expression was set in concrete.

"I guess that brought back memories for you" I said as I handed Nia's nightclothes to her mother. She took her time to put lotion on Nia and to dress her *baby,* like she had done many years ago. The sight of Nia being taken care of by her mother brought a stronger sense of what might have been if we, her mother and I, would have handled ourselves with Nia in mind.

Through careful analysis and self-examination and talking to everyone under the sun, I developed a philosophy that would help me make sense of what would never make sense. I told myself not to dwell on the events of my past because there was nothing in the past I shared with Nia's mother that should be rehashed. Seeing her mother again brought up memories that should have been missing along with Jimmy Hoffa. The memories her mother experienced were different from my own.

"I remember how Nia would splash in the tub" her mother said in a joyful voice. We then began a long and very detailed conversation based on the "remember when" questions. The recall conversation steered clear of the negative that was our lives together. Time passed and it was time for her mother to leave in order for Nia and me to get some much-needed sleep.

"What time will you be back in the morning?" I asked as I walked her mother to the door.

"I will be back in the morning at 9 a.m." she answered. She paused in thought then amended her thought.

"Is 9 a.m. too early for Nia?"

"Heck no, that chick will be up about 6 a.m."

"She still gets up early in the morning."

"Yes, she does much to my chagrin."

"I will be here at 9 a.m." she said as she walked through the door but not before she wished me a good night. I closed the door and headed for the bathroom.

The Big Mack I ate wanted to make a cameo appearance. After my sit on the porcelain throne, I took a long warm shower then hopped on the bed. Nia was long asleep in her bed by the time I jumped under the covers: but for me, sleep was hard to fall upon me. I thrashed about the bed unable to find a comfortable position to force sleep to come. It wasn't until I noticed that my legs trembled and my stomach began to catch wings did I realize the true nature of my insomnia.

The years of living alone with Nia had me anticipate what my first encounter with Nia's mother would be like. All the events of the past had made us nothing more than casual friends who decided to meet for lunch. As soon as the lunch ended they went about their day with very little thought about each other. I fell asleep to the thought that Nia deserved better than distance parents and somehow, I was going to make it better for her.

CHAPTER 28

Morning came and brought me a clearer mind than the day prior. My thoughts were not of the long ago rather I thought first about Nia and trying to help her process what would happen later in the day.

"We are going back home today" I said to Nia upon her exit from the bathroom after taking her morning shower. The trip was planned as an overnight venture because I did not know what to expect from her mother and from Nia. My greatest apprehension about the trip was how Nia would react first to seeing her mother, then separating from her. Obviously, Nia could not talk; however, her silence by no means indicated a lack of understanding and feelings concerning the situation. The smile Nia gave me after I made the pronouncement was enough to know that seeing her mother again did not traumatize her. "Do you remember your mother?" I foolishly asked because it was clear from her reaction the night before Nia did. Nia looked at me and laughed. I took her laughter as an affirmation to my question.

At 9 a.m. sharp, Nia's mother arrived to take us to breakfast then to her apartment. Her timing was impeccable because Nia was getting restless. Her regular television programming was not the same in the south. She could not find her favorite shows on the television. Nia's mother drove us to the nearby Waffle House, a staple of southern breakfast excellence. During the drive, I asked her mother about the vehicle she drove. I should have remembered the old adage about asking questions and the possible answers.

"This is the third car I had. I got the first one within a month of moving here" she said as she drove down the state route named, Po White Highway. I knew we were in the south, but there could not have been a real person with the last name "Po White." After I got over the name, I realized that Nia's mother owned a car and had her own apartment and I had neither. I made considerably more money than she did, but I was unable to do anything more than take care of necessities: but I made my bed.

Nia's mother gave us a tour of her apartment which was rather nice. She lived in a one-bedroom apartment in a quiet complex. It was a little weird to have not known anything about her mother's life since we separated, except for where she worked. I looked around her apartment and there was no sign of anyone living with her. There may have been a man in her life but there was no outward sign. Nia was not looking for anything other than playing in her mother's shoes she left by the bedside. Nia found the pillow on the bed and tossed it down on the floor to play her favorite game with her unsuspecting mother.

"You pick it up right now!" Nia playfully said to her mother about the pillow. It was the same game Nia first played with my mother. Her mother did not need any translation for Nia spoke clear as day. Her mother did not know what to make of Nia's pillow toss until I schooled her.

"Oh, my baby said that loud and clear" her mother said and she told Nia to "Pick up the pillow." Nia picked it up and laughed loudly. I shook my head when no sooner than Nia picked the pillow up she tossed it down to the floor again. The smile on Nia's face pleased both her mother and me. She was truly an innocent and no matter what happened between her parents, Nia was happy to have us both in the same place.

The stay at her apartment was a melancholy experience because once we left; Nia's mother drove us to the hotel room. It was time for Nia and me to leave and there was the potential for a sad departure. The last time Nia saw her mother in New York City was such a situation, when my presence ended a tug-o-war between Nia's mother and my mother. Nia was young at that time and hopefully did not remember; if it happened again there would be no way she would not remember. My fears would prove to be unfounded.

As we stood in front of the car Nia held her mother's hand tightly. She giggled as she knew she was about to take another long car ride home and because she held her mother's hand.

"Tell your mother you will see her later" I told Nia who did as she was told with and went one better, she gave her mother a kiss on the forehead. Her mother gave Nia a big hug and returned the kiss and upped the ante with an even bigger hug. I opened the door and Nia jumped in the front seat of the car and looked to turn on the car radio. She could not because I had the car keys, therefore, she looked at herself in the vanity mirror. Her mother and I were alone and neither of us could say anything more than what needed to be said to each other.

"You did a fantastic job raising Nia. She is so beautiful" her mother said with a sad voice. I did not want this to turn into a cry-fest, therefore, I looked to defer her comments.

"I did the best I could" I answered.

"Thank you for bringing my baby to see me. Don't' be a stranger."

She spoke in an upbeat voice but there had to be a wave of emotion running heavy just beneath the surface. I had to get out of town before my drive back would make me an emotional wreck. I don't remember if I gave her mother a hug before I entered the car, but I feel that in my emotional state at the time I hope I did. Everything after that is a blur to me. I cannot honestly say what happened when I pulled off away from Nia's mother.

In an instant, it was all over. Nia saw her mother for the first time in six years, and there were no hard feelings between any of the parties involved. I wanted this trip to be the first of many but events unforeseen would keep Nia away from her mother longer than six years.

WHOSE BUSINESS IS IT

This story is just my side of what happened. It's a one-dimensional depiction of complex issues and without her mother's point of view, my account can be considered biased. Jesus said it best, "Let him without sin cast the first stone!"

I made my apologies to Nia's mother and she made hers to the Lord. I care not to illuminate the subject in great detail in this book. The subject is key to Nia's life, and since she cannot talk it would be unfair to say things that her mother can neither confirm nor deny.

CHAPTER 29

Nia could have been a radio DJ on any top 40 station. On those types of stations, they play the same songs all day every day. She played the same song over the car stereo as she did on the way down to see her mother. It got so that I made her play something else for the first hour of the trip home. Driving with Nia was almost like driving alone. She was there with me in the car, but she could not talk to me. The lack of a two-way conversation left me to sing aloud and unfortunately think to myself.

I promised Perky that I would visit him in his new home. He recently married his longtime girlfriend and bought a home for her and her daughter. There was joy in his voice with the idea of my brief visit to his new acquisition, there was a little doubt on my part because I was the lone driver. I called Perky on my cell phone once I crossed over into Maryland, and the sound of his voice convinced me to make a quick stop against my fear of what waited up the highway for me.

Nia continued to play DJ on the car stereo and eventually, she returned to playing the same song she played for most of the trip down to see her mother. Her repetitiveness annoyed me, but what really got my goat was that I did not like the song at first but I learned to like the song.

I turned off the Interstate and onto another road once I realized I was lost. I called Perky and he confirmed that I was very lost. In the middle of trying to put me back on the right road the urge to go to the bathroom came upon me. Where to go and what to do with Nia while I relieved myself took control. After driving around for more than twenty minutes I found a strip mall and a store I could see that had a bathroom. I quickly pulled into the first parking space I found nearly hitting a cat that happened to run past.

In the time it took for me to cut off the engine, I debated leaving Nia in the car while I ran inside. I quickly decided against it and brought Nia with me inside the store. Inside the store, I came upon a female worker who I sized up in a nanosecond. Nia was still too young for me to simply tell her to "stay put," so I walked up to the woman and with fear in my eyes and trust that I made a good decision.

"Could you watch her for a moment while I use the restroom?" "She does not speak" I begged. The woman took pity on me and took hold of Nia.

"If she wants something, please give it to her."

The woman took Nia from me and I slipped into the bathroom. I had to go in the worst way, but I took as little time as possible. I could imagine Nia flopping all over the floor or stripping off her clothes in my absence. I nervously washed my hands and rushed out to find that Nia made out like a bandit. She had candy, potato chips and cheese doodles in her arms. The female store worker looked at me and said with a straight face.

"I think she wants all of this" she said as she pointed out all the goodies Nia wanted. Nia giggled heartily as she saw the stunned look on my face. She had gotten away with murder with me. She did not do any of the horrible things I thought she would when I was in the bathroom.

"It's alright." "She can have it all" I said as I reached into my pocket to pay for the candy despite my reluctance to have her eat candy, because of the fact that we would be away from home for another six hours. I should have stuck to my guns.

We left Perky's beautiful house after spending two hours there. I got to meet his lovely wife but I did not meet their daughter. We would have stayed for one of Perky's famous seafood dinners, but the sugar kicked in on Nia. She could not sit still, and after she put her shoes on his wife's white sofa. I decided to leave before we caused trouble for my friend. We left with the sun hanging low in the sky, which was not the way I wanted it to be when I reached South Jersey.

I crossed the Delaware Memorial Bridge and entered the Garden State just as the day sky gave way to the night sky. The well-lit interstate highway gave way to a two-lane highway crowded by trees on either side. It was as dark as any road I traveled in the Northeast. I hated this stretch of road because the darkness made me focus on the road ahead with much more importance. There was nothing to break up the darkness, and I was already tired; and this stretch of road would only increase my fatigue. There was nothing for me to do but drive and stay awake. Staying awake was something Nia could not manage.

Upon entering New Jersey, I realized that Nia had not changed the song for five miles. I took a quick glance over to her to see that she was fast asleep. She stayed awake as long as she could, but the long ride in the car finally did what all the excitement of the day could not. My eyes were getting heavy and I could not blast music to keep me awake because it would disturb Nia's rest.

My best recourse was to periodically roll down the window to get some cool air. When the window was up I talked to myself. For the next two hours, the time it took me to exit New Jersey I had a long and loud conversation with myself. The main topic of my conversation was Nia and her mother.

I pulled into my block and was lucky to find another parking spot right in front of the building. Nia woke up out of her sleep as soon as I completed parking the car. Immediately I gathered up as much as I could carry and escorted Nia upstairs to the apartment. When I walked through the door my mother was in the middle of cursing out Derek Jeter for making a rare error at shortstop. She turned her attention away from those Damn Yankees and onto her returning housemates.

"How did it go on your trip?" my mother asked as she left the couch to give her tired grandchild a kiss on the forehead.

"It went well. I will give you more details after I get Nia into the tub" I said to my mother before I led Nia down the hall to the bathroom. Nia ran towards her delayed 8 p.m. bath. My long-awaited meeting with Nia's mother had gone better than I ever imagined.

In the years that we were separated, my thoughts were a fertile ground for the devil to do his work on me. Every scenario I conjured up in my idle mind looked to set the score straight, on what I thought about what went on between her and Nia. All the time and energy that was spent on plans were a waste. I could have better spent my time thinking about better days and not sour nights. Seeing Nia's mother was the best cure for what ailed me. However and more importantly, I could not say what Nia felt about the meeting.

MIRROR TO HER SOUL

Finally having the chance to turn that proverbial page in my life lifted me to the highest heights as a parent. The visit began my long travail towards redemption and repentance. During the trip back to New York, as well as during the days after the trip to see her mother, I often thought what Nia took away from the brief visit with her mother and what effect it had on her.

Parents of special needs children must keep in mind how events will resonate with their child forever more. Whether the event is positive or negative the experience and its handling are key for development. There are some situations one should never place their child in: but the children grow.

At a young age, Nia did not like loud noises. She would place her fingers in her ears and hum as means of canceling out the affronting noises. In time Nia became less sensitive to loud noises due to my pushing the envelope. I did not avoid the loud noises, instead I limited her exposure to them. Nia built a tolerance for the noise. I learned the signals to how loud noises affected her. My understanding came when I began to start to see things through her eyes.

Special Needs children have their moments as do all children: but we have to keep that in mind. They may not understand what you want from them or the situation especially if there is danger involved. We see the danger with standing near the edge, but *they* the special needs child might only see the shiny object below. Our job is to keep an eye on the child: but at the same time understand that they do have challenges, and they should not be expected to see what it is we see. The key to this is understanding the individual.

Knowing the child means a connection has been made. If the parent or guardian thinks of *self*-first and not as the child sees the world around them, and demands that the child do what they say as soon as the order is issued, then frustration will not be far behind. Actions or words of the child would not equal the punishment doled out by the angry adult. A frustrated parent in the presence of any child for a prolonged period of time is a conflict waiting to occur.

No one has all the answers and not everyone acts their best twenty-four-seven when around children. But when it comes to children who may have the mental capacity of an infant, some things will have to be overlooked if a bigger goal the parent set is to be met. Expecting the child to act with in their *disabilities set,* and not as we want them too all the time is a good start. Having the child experience different things may not result in behaviors that are proper for the moment, but it will help all parties grow together. In order for the child and the parent to grow there have to be some expectations; thus the war will begin in earnest.

CHAPTER 30

"Knowing is half the battle."

This was a well-spoken phrase heard by me from the adults I lived around, who uttered this on more than one occasion. The meaning of the phrase was lost to me during my younger years. As I grew into an adult the meaning of the phrase came to me as a singular thought. Once I knew what I knew, the most difficult part was putting the knowledge to good use.

I did right by Nia but I had to do the same for myself by taking Nia to see her mother. There were many things I wanted to do in life with Nia and without her. One of the things I wanted to do was to have more time to myself. Weekends at YAI were one thing, but I needed time away from Nia and she needed time away from me. The best way for us to get away from each other was for Nia to attend sleep-away summer camp.

I was encouraged to attend a summer camp fair for special needs children. The idea of sending Nia to camp away from my eyes was a tough decision for me: but felt that I was on a roll that had to continue until my changes proved to be a mistake.

Choosing a summer camp at the informal fair setting was difficult for me. As I dragged Nia from one exhibit to another she had no understanding of our purpose there. She happily collected pamphlets to create collages once we made it home. I, on the other hand, could not discern one camp from another. My anguish stemmed from my tunnel vision on the camp's proximity to water and the overall safety of Nia. I relayed my fears to each person manning the exhibits and they supplied me with the same response.

"Our camp is staffed by concerned adults. The camper's safety is our first concern."

Their words did little to relieve my fears, but once again I was on a roll of change. I simply closed my eyes and made the best-informed choice I could under the circumstances. One solid week away from Nia did my soul good. There was no phone call from the camp to tell me to pick Nia up early like there was from YAI. Whatever she was doing was well within moderate behavior, which was all right with me. When I left Nia on the bus she left me with a smile. When she returned from camp she returned with a smile; but unbeknownst to me, Nia was not the same person she was just one week earlier.

Nia was more than happy to see me at the pickup site. She laughed and even gave me a kiss on the check, which was a rarity for her. I was happier to see her than she was to see me. I asked the counselor who was with Nia at the camp about her behavior and she had nothing but praise for my daughter. The praise surprised me because I did expect them to tell me she had trouble sleeping or at least threw a tantrum. She did not make mention of anything happening out of the normal, thus I was extremely surprised when I got her home.

We returned home to a warm welcome from my mother. Nia gave my mother a quick wave and a low audible understood "Hello" and she darted towards the back of the apartment and her room. As my mother and I talked in the living room, I watched Nia enter and exit the bathroom. Her quick in and out meant that she had not wiped herself well after using the bathroom sometime earlier in the day.

Nia had the habit of changing her soiled underwear for a clean pair, but she would leave the soiled pair in the sink. She saw me more than once cleaning her underwear in the sink, therefore, she knew part of the process but not the most convenient one for me. After chatting with my mother for a few more minutes before I went to the bathroom to clean up after Nia. Upon entering the bathroom, what I saw stunned me.

Nia did, in fact, change her underwear but I noticed something that looked like an adult diaper wedged in her underwear.

"What the shit is this?" I said to myself as I removed the adult diaper from the underwear. When I took a closer look at the adult diaper I saw something in it that rocked me to my core. The counselor said nothing out of the ordinary happened to Nia when she was in camp. However, the counselor did not mention that my little girl had grown into a young lady at the age of twelve while she was at camp. I was devastated, because of the shroud of ignorance, I hid behind.

This day was inevitable, but it was one that I could not face until there was no escape from its clutches. I walked towards the living room as if I walked to my death. Each step brought me closer to another moment where I put myself before my child. I told my mother and she once again said what I needed to hear.

"You knew it would happen and you know what you have to do" my mother said to me. I picked up my wallet and headed to the store to buy the one thing I never wanted to buy. For a man to buy that *special* item, it was like he lost a notch on his manhood. I did not have to go to the store for my wife or girlfriend. I went to the store for my child who could not go for herself.

I walked into the corner store owned by two brothers and run by their family. Ali was the more recognized of the two. We even called the store "Al's after the brother. He was the most vocal and sometimes more direct, while his brother Abdul was very laid back and personable. It was Abdul behind the counter when I placed the package on the counter along with a bottle of Ole English Malt Liquor. Abdul saw my face and did not connect the alcohol with me.

"What's the matter?" Abdul said as he looked at my sullen face. I stuttered for an answer to his pointed question.

"This is … for my … daughter."

I said as I pointed meekly at the package on the counter in front of me. Abdul looked at me with his brown eyes and said what my mother did in another way.

"It's life. What are you gonna' do?" Abdul said as he pulled the bottle away from me and left it on the other side of the counter out of my reach. From that moment on, I no longer worried about what stood in my future with Nia. There was no hiding in a bottle or any other distraction that would take my thoughts off the master plan. Nia was my focus.

I Can't Speak For You

Nia's change from adolescence to teenager was a long adjustment period for me. I had to place marks on calendars for its "friendly" approach and I had to make sure that all her supplies were on hand when it did show its face. With all I had to go through the change must have caused Nia to pause in thought.

Looking into the prism of her mind, Nia had to have questions about the change that took place in her. In spite of her disability Nia had to know that she as growing older and that her life would never be the same. Nia unable to speak with her mouth must have wanted to ask many questions but she was trapped in a mind that had little connection to the outside world. Information flowed stronger in one direction towards Nia and not out towards the world.

Communication is the most important part of any relationship, without it there is no way of forming a bond that would last through troubled times. For all of Nia's life, I would ask her the same basic questions hoping that she would one day be able to express her feelings.

"How are you doing?"

"What do you want to eat?"

"Do you understand what I just told you?"

The most difficult part of raising Nia was to have to think for her every day. I decided what she was to eat, wear and every other function any teenager would do themselves. What made it difficult was that I might have to do the same for the rest of her life. The thought of that did not sit well with me. I had to take action, or Nia may never reach her optimal potential.

I decided to give Nia as much freedom as possible. I asked her to pick out her clothes until she was able to decide for herself what she wanted to wear that day. Very quickly and to my surprise she would pick out items that matched. I continued to supervise her but it thrilled me to learn that she did have a preference. She had a capacity to grow and I had to push the envelope within reason to see how far she could go. Try to push and one might fail: but the possibility of success outweighed any failure.

CHAPTER 31

Over and over again I praised God for my family; for without them I would have been lost long before Nia entered puberty. The best time for me was when we gathered each Thanksgiving at alternate apartments. The food and the loud banter of the celebration were worth the wait. During one such gathering, Nia took all by storm.

The day was joyous but at the same time somber because many of the people that saw me in my youth never had the opportunity to see me as a father to Nia. I sometimes thought how Nia would react to my father when he was healthy. The imaginary sight of each of my grandmothers bouncing Nia on their tender knees always brought smiles to my face. I often thought of how much Nia would like the food prepared on Thanksgiving.

During my childhood my father and my maternal grandmother would prepare the entire meal for upwards of forty people, with minimal help from those forty people! I stood in the doorway to my kitchen while the smells and sights of old came to my mind's eye. The image I had of my father and grandmother working the kitchen was superimposed over what took place in the kitchen. The voice of my cousin Joanne stripped the second layer of the image in my mind away leaving me with the present.

"You're standing there ain't gonna' make the food come any faster."

Joanne said to me and as I awoke from my thoughts. I did not realize how long I stood there and I was slightly embarrassed therefore the best thing to do was to tell her what had me staring dumbly into space.

"I was just thinking about Daddy and Grandma." I said as I was handed a pan of baked macaroni by Joanne.

"While you're thinking about them, put that on the table" she ordered as she handed me the pan and I followed instructions and returned to the kitchen to find that my statement had caused a discussion about my grandmother and father.

"I miss my daddy" my sister Debra said about our father. My aunt Joyce who was also in the kitchen had her own recollections.

"If my mother Vinita and Reggie were alive we would have been at the table eating already" she sarcastically said, since everyone had to prepare and bring his or her best dishes: and sometimes people arrive late. This Thanksgiving was no exception.

Every one of the people who entered the apartment made it a point to greet everyone who was present, and they made sure to greet Nia who looked away until she was prompted to speak. Nia spoke and then made her way over to the couch where she sat for most of the night. Nia was not acting like herself, she did not do the things she used to do to draw attention to herself. Instead Nia sat on the couch reading the lips of everyone in the room. It was as if she were sitting for rehearsal during the plays she wanted to take part in the conversations, she did not know how. Once the food was placed on the table all the conversations stopped. Talking and eating did not go well together.

As usual, I was told to come back only once for food but this year my younger cousin J. B. and my great nephew Brett could eat everyone out of house and home. I waited patiently for everyone to fill their plates before stepping up to my plate at the table. I piled up my plate with lasagna, macaroni and cheese, collard greens and anything else that would fit on my plate. I took one bite of the ham and my stomach yelled in glee. As I was about to take another bite of food Nia yelled out.

Her yell was profound enough that it caused everyone in the living room to take notice. I rested my fork on my mound of food and moved towards Nia but my cousin Joanne beat me to Nia.

"What's the matter?" he asked Nia. Her question was met with another scream from. Nia sat at the table where all the food was found and I did not make sure she did not want anything to eat.

"I would be mad too if everybody but me was eating" my cousin Alenda said with a hearty laugh. Many of my family members say Nia and Alenda look alike, they may look alike but all I see in Nia is her mother. For the next five minutes, everyone took turns letting me know that I forgot about Nia but she spoke up for herself, which was a first for her. She sat and ate several helpings of ham never once moving from the table. Nia had made a huge step forward and I could not have been any prouder of her.

Thanksgiving proved to be a pivotal period in Nia's upbringing. She began to come out of her own world and introduce herself to the environment. There would be another gathering where Nia would have a chance to display her social skills.

CHAPTER 32

I could not help but beam with a sense of deep pride as I waited long with Nia for the bus to whisk her off to her Saturday program. Her hair flowed down to her shoulders in thick braids done by Leah the prior night. My little girl on this day was nine years old and for a brief moment, I marveled at how much she had grown. Ms. Wynn, another longtime resident of *310* entered the building after doing some food shopping at the local Supermarket. Every time she saw Nia Ms. Wynn spoke to Nia and sometimes Nia would give her a fast response to "Hi" before she would go off into her own world. This never deterred the mother of four from greeting Nia.

"Hey Nia, I heard today is your birthday? Happy birthday Nia!" Ms. Wynn said as she pulled her shopping cart loaded with groceries into the vestibule of the building.

"How is your mother Darryl?" she added as she placed her key in the door of the lobby. I pulled her shopping cart out of the way of the opening door and responded to her question.

"My mother is doing fine."

"How are Jackie and her twins?"

"She is fine, they are loveable pains in the neck."

"They are getting so big. How does Nia get along with them?"

"Nia is Nia. As long as she has Barney on T.V. she is in her own world" I answered as she pulled the oft-broken door open with her foot and held it.

"What do you have planned for her today?" he asked as I pushed her cart through the door and into the lobby.

"I am having a bowling party for her this afternoon" I answered as I held the door open with my foot. "Have a good time Nia" she declared as she disappeared into the lobby. I turned to find Nia left the vestibule and was not outside in the cool morning air. Nia was famous for making her move whenever I was in conversation or distracted by something. I was lucky because when she was younger she could lie on the ground or laugh hysterically to get my attention. It was refreshing to find she could act in a different way. Nia's quiet wait turned into her impatiently whining and humming as the bus was a few minutes late. Just when she was about to have a tantrum the little yellow lifesaver turned the corner.

The driver opened the door and the bus matron in her thick Caribbean accent greeted us. I never asked her where she was born. I would let the mystery unfold naturally.

"Good morning Mr. Lawson how are you, Nia?" she asked as Nis escorted Nia onto the bus.

"Today is Nia's birthday and I will pick her up early from the program" I said in succession.

"Oh, I wish you would have told me I would have gotten her something" she responded. The door closed and Nia was off to her program. I had several things to do before the party that afternoon and there was little time to get it done.

After running errands, I made it back to the apartment to pick up my mother and the birthday cake. We picked Nia up from her program and took her on a train ride to the Port Authority Bus Terminal on the famed 42nd Street for her special day. There were only a few places left to bowl on Manhattan Island and the bowling alley located inside the terminal was the best of the bunch. We arrived just in time to greet the guests.

Ms. Underwood came with her daughter and Armando brought three of his children. Ms. Williams, Killer and his new girlfriend Dee arrived as well. Kevin called but like always he was on the road driving south to see family. My Aunt Audrey and her daughter Donna came. Uncle Charlie was not feeling well and Donna's children stayed with him. My sister Debra came in from Delaware along with her husband Larry. Cleve was there with his girlfriend and her child who was the same age as Nia. In all, there must have been fifty people there to support Nia on her big day. I wished my father could have been there to see the love everyone had for Nia. My auntie Joyce walked through the door and got the party started as no other could.

I made sure Nia had a chance to bowl which she did until she got hold of French fries and pizza and that was the end of the bowling experience. I was happy when Jeffery and his wife Kim walked through the door along with their daughter Jayla. The only family missing were the family members that lived out of town. It was a big moment for me to share a big day with many of the people who helped keep me sane.

My mother sat next to me and she must have been in my mind at that point. She tapped me on my leg as she did before she imparted words of wisdom.

"You did good Darryl. You may not have everything you want but God has given you everything you need."

She conveyed to me. My mother knew there were many things I wanted to do like take a vacation out of the country and buy a car. The car would be my freedom to travel and see the people I had not seen with any frequency, like my sister Kim in New Jersey and her kids. It would have also marked a point in my financial life that I was able to do more than just dream.

"I know Mother. He gave me you didn't he" I replied as I laughed inwardly as one of the twins rolled a strike and shouted one of my lines from my sister's plays.

"I am somebody. Scooby-Doobie Doo!"

I shook my head at the fact he remembered my line from the play five years ago. The approach of my nephew Brett interrupted my thoughts.

"Uncle Darryl, my mother said it's time to cut the cake" se shyly said. He was two years older than Nia and his sister Jazmine. My Aunts Joyce and Audrey sat nearby and commented on the slow progress of cutting the cake.

"You better cut that cake before I become a year older" my Aunt Audrey quipped.

"He forgot we are in our seventies and I need my beauty sleep" my Aunt Audrey chimed in after my Aunt Joyce. I got the hint and rounded up everyone and walked Nia and my mother over to the cake. While my niece Vonnetta started to light the cake I got a text from

Levine that he and Ennis would not be able to make the party. Their presence would have increased my friendship circle but there would be another day. Vonnie lit the candles on the cake, which upon it was written Happy Birthday Nia and Debra in pink and purple lettering. The gathering began to sing Stevie Wonder's birthday song to Martin Luther King Junior and before the song was over Nia smiled and clapped her hands. She was present during many birthday celebrations and knew what it was like to show praise of another year on someone.

"Look at her smile" my mother exclaimed. It was the first time Nia understood when she was the center of attention and ate it up. She blew out the candles before the song was done but it was acceptable. Everyone laughed as she continued to clap her hands as she bubbled with excitement. Everyone there accepted Nia for what she was and in turn, she let us all know what she thought about us.

CHAPTER 33

I awoke from a rare long night's sleep feeling as if I had just made my way into my bed. My lack of sleep took me back to the time when Nia was a young girl living in *1199*, when restful sleep for me was rare as a pink diamond. I did not want to get out of the bed because it would mean the start of my day began.

The day before had been usually long. I had to leave work early to run Nia to her dental appointment: then uptown to the doctor to fill out paperwork for her new after-school program. The running wore me out; but grading papers into the wee hours of the morning made going to work a bitter pill for me to swallow. I was always on the move running from here to there all for Nia, but this day I did not want to start a new day whose limits may be above my will to sustain.

After convincing myself to get out of bed, I placed my feet on the purple carpet my sister left behind. I toyed with the idea of staying at home but as always, I talked myself out of doing something for me for the sake of my students. I had work I needed to return and not giving it to them would bring up a sense of guilt. Going to work gave me the chance to ease my worries about Nia.

Feeling my feet firmly planted on the carpet put my day into perpetual motion. I glanced over at the clock on the cable box for the time. (Gone were the days of clock radios for telling time the cable box did the same without blurting out loud tones.) I looked over at my computer that lay in the right-hand corner of the room. Nia played her game just before she went to bed but I was too tired to cut it off before going to bed. The blue screen illuminating the room did not allow for my accustomed darkness to enter the place. It was not until I realized the computer might have helped to take the sleep from me.

I made my way over to the computer and on the computer stand laid a copy of my first published book titled "Trouble Comes In 3's." It was a twenty-year endeavor to create the Great American Novel. Looking at the book with Cleve' Sonny Chiba and Nathan on the cover gave me a strong sense of pride I lacked for many years.

Trouble Comes In 3's was going to be the first book in a series written by me that would give me a new revenue stream, that would give me the financial stability I needed. Finishing what I started many years in the past was just one accomplishment I set my sights on achieving. I walked over to the window and peered out through the fleeting night sky at the parking lot below. I was giddy enough to literally pinch myself, for in parking spot number twenty-eight was my forty-second birthday present to me a Cadillac CTS. It was not the Callaway modified Corvette of my dreams, but my first car was a real car.

"Damn I did well" I said aloud as I opened the draws and pulled out my socks and underwear to wear for that day. After I closed the draws once again I glanced down at my shiny blue car. I left my room and made my way to the shower, but no sooner than the sound of my door opening Nia began to make her noises in the bed with my mother. The instant I got out the shower Nia tried to push passed] me and into the bathroom. I blocked her path and made her speak to me.

"Say good morning and excuse me" I demanded as I made sure my towel did not fall off my waist.

"Good morning" she said in her best possible language. There was no way I was going to move until she greeted me. I went directly to my room to get dressed. This was one of the rare mornings where I ironed both Nia and my clothes the night before. I emerged from my room fully dressed. Nia was still in the shower which was not a problem; because it gave me time to make her favorite breakfast of the day grits and sausage. As I passed the bathroom I could hear the water running but I could hear her speaking, making her funny noises in the bathroom. The sound of her voice from behind the door was very familiar to me. She had to be standing up in the tub, which meant she turned that water hot in the tub. The water was not just hot but scalding hot, enough to turn her light brown skin beet red. Often when she took baths I checked on her to make sure that she did not do the dangerous act. I disliked peeking in on her given her age, but I had to keep her safe.

"Nia turn the cold water on" I said to her after I knocked on the door before I entered the bathroom. I waited long enough to see that she turned the water down before I closed the door and went on to the kitchen. As I passed my mother's room I closed her door to give her more time to sleep before she had to go to church and feed the homeless later that morning.

As always, I had to stop cooking to chase Nia out of the bathroom or we would be late for the bus. She was able to dress, however; she needed help with tying her shoes and putting on her belt. As soon as she was dressed Nia sat down to eat breakfast, after which I was made to suffer through Barney each and every morning at the same time. I washed the dishes then hurriedly signed trip slips I was unable to detect the prior night. I brushed her teeth as well as my own and this morning I was happy to remember to put deodorant on Nia. My mistake caused my child to go to school smelling like a man on more than one occasion.

"You have to remind me to put deodorant on you, Nia" I said to her but of course, she would not answer. I put on our coats and headed for the front door. The school bus was scheduled to come in ten minutes. I gathered up the garbage to drop it down the compactor chute. Just before I closed the door behind me I realized that I had left my keys inside.

"Nia put the garbage down the chute" I handed the garbage to her as I recovered my apartment keys. Nia went about the task as directed and I picked up my apartment keys and for some reason my car keys. I had not driven my car to work since I brought it home, but I had thought it would be a good idea to carry the keys anyway.

We boarded the elevator making sure to sidestep the usual chicken bones and empty cups on the floor. The dirty elevator was too much to fathom that early in the day. The elevator arrived at the lobby and Nia and I stepped out to be greeted by the security guard Monroe who took over the morning shift after Rahim retired.

"Your bus just left" Monroe announced to me. Once more I had a problem with the new bus. The city under Mighty Mouth leader, decided to change the bus driver and matron in January, which wreaked havoc on my schedule.

"He told me he would be here at 7:15 a.m. Monroe. complained to him but I had to complain to the bus company.

"He could have called your house but he did not stay but two minutes" Monroe said.

"I guess I will take her to school" I said as I began to think about the fastest route to her school on the other side of Manhattan from my job. The bus was not practical and taking the train would mean I would have to hope that Nia would be able to get a seat on the train or she would act out. No matter what train I took there would be a bus ride at the end of the journey. Either case being late to work was a real possibility. It came to me that I had a third choice to get to work and it would be to drive her to her school then drive myself to my job.

I called the school and spoke to Holiday, informing her that I might be late for work. She took the message and made arrangements for my being late to work just in case. As I walked Nia to the parking lot I began to think back to how far I had come in my job of raising Nia, and how far I had to go. There would be many more experiences I would have to go through with Nia; but she was My Nia and my purpose for living, and my reason to be a better man.

(And It Continues…)

Made in the
USA
Lexington, KY